# F**ked My Way Up To The Top

## THE COMPLETE BIOGRAPHY OF

# LANA DEL REY

### USING HER OWN WORDS

*F\*\*ked My Way Up to the Top: The Complete Biography of Lana Del Rey Using Her Own Words*
by Jared Woods
co-editing by Milz Dechnik
Published by The Goat's Nest Publishing
ISBN 9798386871697
**JaredWoodsSavedMyLife.com**

"It's commentary, like, 'I know what you think of me', and I'm alluding to that. You know, I have slept with a lot of guys in the industry, but none of them helped me get my record deals. Which is annoying." [1]

**- LANA DEL REY**

# TABLE OF CONTENTS

# INTRODUCTION
# THE ENDURANCE
# OF THE SAD FLOWER

The Elizabeth Woolridge Grant seedling demanded the precise combination of sunshine and shade to flourish within her signature soil. As she struggled to transform into the artistic product her insides cried for, she pursued and discarded a spectrum of petals until she could pluck the perfect nutrients of inspiration from the moody sky.

What eventually pushed up from the dirt as the Lana Del Rey we see today is owed to a number of ethereal specifics. The hunger for bad boys, irrespective of mistreatment. The nostalgic glamour of monochrome cinematic aesthetics. But above every muse, it was the gravitational lore of the American culture that spun Lizzy's creativity up to the stars. The gritty desaturation of New York's commotion. The colourful optimism of Los Angeles' daydreams. The Americana abstraction where the terrain itself became the main character in a growing girl's story.

The concluding blossom was a dark rose surviving through the cracks of a busy sidewalk. It seductively smoked on a cigarette, detached from the real world, weighed heavy by its sultry rebellion whilst wilting itself on purpose. And there she was: the saddest flower in all the land. Burnt out by melancholia, pouting its lolita naivete, and surrendering to utter self-destruction, be it by the temporary arms of promiscuity, the passenger seats of fast cars, or the unholy allure of drugs and firearms.

And yet, within this trashy display of lost innocence, she maintained a contradictory aroma of retro class, a certain enigmatic sophistication rare in the modern zeitgeist. She mumbled tortured romantic poetics about feminity and escapism, if not to anyone, then to herself, trying to make sense of the grey area where her tragic mind fit into the broader cultural landscape.

The public could no longer ignore this unique spectacle, and the backlash was swift and ruthless. Various malicious hands yanked at her stem, outlining her past in accusations of a fabricated persona. Others criticised her seemingly submissive anti-feminist attitude, misusing her role model podium to undo the hard work so many women had fought to inch forward. But these resentments only worked to further corrupt the corrupted, as Lana dug her roots in and stood her ground, churning the poisonous hatred into stronger material with which to fight the masses.

As the years rolled on, the general temperament softened, subdued by the soft lullabies and then wearied by Lana's determination. Unable to deny the endless talent and unceasing productivity, the opposers were forced to concede that they had lost. No one had the power to tear this rose out. The best anyone could do was to become a rose themselves, and sulk in memory of their former ignorant resistance, ashamed by previous hostility and now consumed by the same gloomy love Lana preached since the beginning.

*Fucked My Way to the Top* is the complete biography of Lana Del Rey. We leave no crevice unexplored and reveal how this flower flourished as a global superstar after battling against an onslaught of odds thrown at her path. We map out this journey using her own words taken from hundreds of interviews while digging deep into her musical output—the place Lana has always felt the most comfortable with sharing personal details.

This book is for Lana, revealing the full story of a true artist hiding within the pop world's darker underbelly. And this is for her diehard fans who prefer to live there too.

"If you are born an artist, you have
no choice but to fight
to stay an artist." [2]

# - LANA DEL REY

# PART ONE
# THE EARLY LIFE OF
# LIZZY GRANT

# 1.1.
# THE GRANT PARENTS

<u>DAD</u>

*"Calling from beyond the grave,*
*I just wanna say, 'Hi, Dad.'"*

# - LANA DEL REY
(LYRICS FROM *RIDE*)

Like most narratives of chronological hierarchy, we commence our tale from the patriarchal branch of the Grant family tree.

Robert England "Rob" Grant Jr was born June 16, 1953, in Evanston, Illinois, to Cynthia Grant and Robert Grant Sr. After graduating from Prescott College in Arizona, he started working as a Grey Group executive copywriter. That is, until the late 90s when he invested in web domains and reportedly earned a ton of money doing so. Depending on who you believe, Grant became a self-made millionaire or even a billionaire, although reports vary.

## MOM

*"I'm not friends with my mother,
but I still love my dad."*

# - LANA DEL REY

(LYRICS FROM *BLACK BATHING SUIT*)

Patricia Ann "Patty" Hill-Grant was born December 23, 1955, in Lake Placid, New York, to Madeline Hill and Donald Hill. After graduating from the (now-closed) Bradford College in Haverhill, Massachusetts, and Syracuse University in Syracuse, New York, she pursued a profession as an account manager, then later changed careers to become a school teacher.

Rob and Patty married on June 12, 1982, at Our Lady of Mount Carmel Roman Catholic Church in New York City. Based on the marriage announcement in the New York Times, the two most likely met at Grey Advertising. They are both of Scottish descent with family roots in Lanarkshire.

*"My mom and my dad, they both like to sing. They have really nice voices."* [3]

# - LANA DEL REY

The two currently reside in Lake Placid, New York. Rob is quite active on social media and occasionally converses with Lana's fans. Both parents have also been spotted with Lana on tour from time to time.

Lana freely offers details about her relationship with her folks. Her fondness for her father is forever displayed via her lyrical content and social media presence. Conversely, her association with her mother is far colder. Patty is mentioned in many of Lana's songs and often unfavourably. Examples can be found in *My Momma* (*"Me and my momma, we don't get along"*), *LA Who Am I to Love You?* (*"I never had a mother, will you let me make the sun my own for now, and the ocean my son?"*), and *Wildflower Wildfire* (*"My father never stepped in when his wife would rage at me, so I ended up awkward but sweet"*). Lana has also previously posted about Mother's Day, calling the time *"challenging"* while acknowledging her *"chosen family"* on that date above her biological one.

## 1.2.
# THE GRANT KIDS

*"I wasn't even born in the '50s, but I feel like I was there."* [4]

## - LANA DEL REY

Three years into their marriage, the first Grant child was born on June 21, 1985, in Manhattan, New York City. Her given name was Elizabeth Woolridge Grant, but we know her better as Lana Del Rey.

When Lana was one year old, the family moved to Lake Placid, New York, where they remained for Lana's entire childhood through adolescence. Her mother became a school teacher and her father worked for a furniture company, although it was only a short time before he shifted his focus to domain investing.

*"Wearing our jewels in the swimming pool, me and my sister just playing it cool under the chemtrails over the country club."*

# - LANA DEL REY

(LYRICS FROM *CHEMTRAILS OVER THE COUNTRY CLUB*)

On November 19, 1987, Lana's younger sister, Caroline "Chuck" Grant, was born. From a young age, Chuck began photographing Lana, and she continued the practice into college, now a professional photographer based in Los Angeles and New York City. Lana has hired Chuck for many of her works moving forward, including various album covers (*Lust for Life, Norman Fucking Rockwell!*, etc.) as well as promotional work throughout Lana's career. Consequently, we will be spending ample time with Chuck as this book progresses.

*"She captures what I consider to be the visual equivalent of what I do sonically [...] Now, after I've met so many famous photographers, her aesthetic and talent still stands out*

as being one of the most interesting and well-developed." [5]

## - LANA DEL REY

The third and final child arrived on March 3, 1993, namely Charles "Charlie" Hill-Grant, the couple's only son. Much like Chuck, Lana included Charlie in plenty of her projects, featuring in the short film *Tropico* (2013) and the music videos for *Ride* (2012), *Fuck It I Love You/The Greatest* (2019), *Let Me Love You Like a Woman* (2020) and *Chemtrails Over The Country Club* (2021). He also directed an interview video for Lana in 2020 for Interview magazine, and was behind the camera in the *Arcadia* music video (2020).

"[My parents] had traditional expectations [for my career] geared towards keeping me safe, [so] most of my musical world was kept under wraps. I don't want to say it was a frivolous prospect, but we have nurses in the family, and teachers, and that was more of a reliable profession." [6]

## - LANA DEL REY

## 1.3.
# A TROUBLED STUDENT

Lana attended the Catholic school St. Agnes during her elementary years, and hints of her future career flickered in the distance as she joined the choir. When it was time for high school, she spent one year where her mother worked, but her rowdy behaviour caused problems.

*"I was misdirecting my energy. I started going out all the time and skipping school a little bit, and yeah, I got in trouble."* [7]

## - LANA DEL REY

Perhaps her most discussed issue was with alcohol, which she turned to whenever existential problems plagued her mental space.

"When I was very young, I was sort of floored by the fact that my mother and my father and everyone I knew was going to die one day, and myself too. I had a sort of a philosophical crisis. I couldn't believe that we were mortal. For some reason, that knowledge sort of overshadowed my experience. I was unhappy for some time. I got into a lot of trouble. I used to drink a lot. That was a hard time in my life." [8]

## - LANA DEL REY

When she was 15, her excessive drinking and discord with teachers compelled her parents to send Lana to the private boarding school Kent School in Connecticut to get sober.

"My parents were worried. I was worried. I knew it was a problem when I liked it more than I liked doing anything else. I was like, I'm fed. I am totally fed. Like, at first, it's fine, and you think you have a dark side—it's exciting—and then you realise the dark side wins every time if you decide to indulge in it. It's also a completely different way of living when you know that. It's like being a different species of person. It was horrific. It was the worst thing that ever happened to me [...] It was everything in the end." [9]

## - LANA DEL REY

# 1.4.
# RELATIONSHIP STATUS:
# GENE CAMPBELL

Lana struggled to find her place in Kent School, but there was one saving figure: a teacher named Eugene "Gene" Campbell, who was only a few years older than Lana and inspired her mind in a more artistic direction.

"I was lonely, but I had this teacher who was my only friend in school. His name was Gene. He read us Leaves of Grass and we read Lolita in class, and it changed my world, which was a really solitary world. I didn't have a connection to anyone in class and when I found these writers, I knew they were my people. [...] He would sign me out and we would listen to Tupac and stuff in his car, and he would teach me about old movies like Citizen Kane. He taught me everything." [10]

# - LANA DEL REY

"In boarding school, to become a teacher, you don't have to have a Masters. I was 15, and he was 22, out of Georgetown. He was young, and at school, you were allowed to take trips out at the weekends. On our driving trips around the Connecticut counties, he introduced me to [Vladimir] Nabokov, [Allen] Ginsberg, [Walt] Whitman, and even Tupac and Biggie. He was my gateway to inspirational culture. Those inspirations I got when I was 15 are still my only inspirations. I draw from that same well. It's one world I dip into to create other worlds. Like this philosopher Josiah Royce once said: 'Without the roots, you can't have any fruits.'" [11]

## - LANA DEL REY

Based on these types of interviews, many have questioned the appropriateness of Lana's relationship with this authority figure who was seven years her senior. Lana's unreleased track *Prom Song (Gone Wrong)* is said to be about Gene, which includes the lyrics:

"I knew you loved me by the way you looked in second period. I'd see you in the hall like, 'hello, hello'. Up against the wall like, 'let's go, let's go.'

## - LANA DEL REY

(LYRICS FROM *PROM SONG (GONE WRONG)*)

And then there was *Boarding School*, another unreleased song that further fueled the fire with this line:

"Let's do drugs,
make love with our teachers."

# - LANA DEL REY
(LYRICS FROM *BOARDING SCHOOL*)

Neither party has confirmed nor denied the allegations.

## 1.5.
# LANA GOES SOBER

Regardless, Lana kicked her alcohol habit and has remained largely sober and drug-free since then, even if these intoxicated years did influence many themes in her art.

*"I used to drink a lot, and now I don't drink at all. My whole life was the catalyst [for quitting]. It was a mess. I did lose my car, my family's car. That was a catalyst [...] I forgot where I put it!"* [12]

## - LANA DEL REY

That said, she is famous for her smoking aesthetic, a habit she's developed since she was 17 years old and has confessed to an excessive coffee addiction.

"Sugar, coffee. I must have 13 cups a day. It's a shame about the health consequences because a lot of great things happen over coffee and a cigarette. A lot of great songs were written [...] I'm a chain-smoker." [13]

## - LANA DEL REY

# PART TWO
# PRE-LANA ERA

# 2.1.
# POST-GRADUATION

After graduating, Lana moved to Long Island to live with her aunt and uncle for a year. She worked as a waitress but, more importantly, learned some guitar playing from her uncle.

"It was G, C, A. It was D minor, A minor and some diminished chord as well. Some trick, some shortcut. I realised I could probably write a million songs with those six chords—so I moved to New York and I took a

couple of years to just write whatever
I wanted." [14]

## - LANA DEL REY

Lana packed up and relocated to her birth city of NYC at the age of 19. She enrolled in Fordham University in the Bronx to study philosophy with a keen interest in metaphysics.

"[It] bridged the gap between God and
science. I was interested in God and
how technology could bring us closer to
finding out where we came
from and why." [15]

## - LANA DEL REY

# 2.2.
# RELIGION

*"God has saved me a million times."* [16]

## - LANA DEL REY

L ana has since stated she is not religious but *"more spiritual, I know that's a cliché"* which has played a noticeable role in her lyrical influences.

*"I went to a Catholic school called St. Agnes and I loved going to church. I was very interested and curious about the idea of a divine plan and that there was something bigger than us*

out there. I don't have a traditional Catholic view of religion or God though—but I enjoy the feeling of being looked after in the spiritual sense." [17]

## - LANA DEL REY

"I got to a point 10 years ago where everything was so wrong in my personal life that I let go and stopped willing my way into life. When I let go of everything and stopped trying to become a singer and write good songs and be happy, things then fell into place. I was surrendering to life on life's terms. It was this very real experience with a life science that nobody had taught me. You let go of everything you think you want, and focus on everything you love, so it's the only vibration you're putting out there." [18]

## - LANA DEL REY

"I mixed [philosophy] with my studies in theology, because it was the best school for the Jesuit faith and all of the Jesuits taught philosophy classes. There was just a lot of talk about going back to that basic question: Why do we exist? How did reality come to be? Why do we do what we do? And how not to become the butcher, the baker, the candlestick maker, the guardians of the middle-class. That really interested me [...] I loved being around people who wondered why we were here." [19]

# - LANA DEL REY

"I think there's a division of organised religion [...] but where I'm concerned, my understanding of God has come from my own personal experiences, because I was in trouble so many times in New York that if you were me, you would believe in God too. When things get bad enough, your only resort is to lie in bed and start praying. I dunno about congregating once a week in a church and all that, but when I heard there is a divine power you can call on, I did. I suppose my approach to religion is like my approach to music: I take what I want and leave the rest." [20]

# - LANA DEL REY

"One thing you learn when you do get sober is that complete surrender is the foundation for all good things to come. And I feel like that idea translated to all aspects of my life. When you have absolutely no idea what's going to happen to you or what your career's *going to end up like and you're just really open to anything, then you don't really have anything to lose. A lot of different people come in and out of your life. And it's really fun to say yes, and it's really fun to be easy about everything and just let songs come to you and let people come to you. And it is free, in a way."* [21]

## - LANA DEL REY

But while the philosophy side of education was stimulating her mind, it was in Fordham University that her main pursuit in the music community was taking over her attention.

*"That was when my musical experience began. I kind of found people for myself."* [22]

## - LANA DEL REY

# 2.3.
# MAY JAILER

"This is from when I was 17. [I] have
no idea where you got it from."

## - LANA DEL REY

(YOUTUBE COMMENT ON *A STAR FOR NICK*)

While in NYC, Lana took the big step and started per-forming in the nightclub scene under names such as *Sparkle Jump Rope Queen* and *Lizzy Grant and the Phenomena.*

"Yeah, I like jump ropes [...] I do have
actual sparkle jump ropes. I'm a

collector of many things, that is one
of the things." [23]

## - LANA DEL REY

"I was always singing, but didn't plan
on pursuing it seriously. When I got to
New York City when I was eighteen, I
started playing in clubs in Brooklyn—I
have good friends and devoted fans
on the underground scene, but we were
playing for each other at that point—
and that was it." [24]

## - LANA DEL REY

Still in college in 2005, Lana got busy. She registered a seven-track EP with the United States Copyright Office called *Young Like Me* (aka *Rock Me Stable*). Around the same time, she recorded another ten-track project, known as *From the End.*

These remain unreleased, but numerous tracks were leaked in 2014 (often under the unofficial title *Quiet Now.*

## 2.4.
# ALBUM: SIRENS (2006)

# SIRENS (2006)

## 1. Drive By
*(also known as For K (Part 1); found on Young Like Me)*

## 2. Next to Me
*(unconfirmed title, also known as River Road)*

## 3. A Star for Nick

## 4. My Momma
*(unconfirmed title)*

## 5. Bad Disease
*(found on From the end.)*

## 6. Out with a Bang
*(found on From the end.)*

## 7. Dear Elliot
*(found on From the end.; also known as Westbound)*

## 8. Try Tonight
*(found on From the end.)*

## 9. Peace
*(found on From the end.; also known as All You Need)*

## 10. How Do You Know Me so Well?
*(also known as I'm Indebted to You; found on From the end.)*

## 11. Pretty Baby
*(unconfirmed title)*

## 12. Aviation
*(found on From the end.)*

## 13. Move
*(also known as Find My Own Way; found on Young Like Me)*

## 14. Junky Pride
*(alternatively spelt as Junkie Pride; found on Young Like Me)*

## 15. Birds of a Feather
*(unconfirmed title)*

# TOTAL RUNTIME: 53:17

Ten of the songs from the aforementioned projects were demos that ultimately made her unreleased acoustic album *Sirens* under Del Rey's then-stage name, *May Jailer*. Recorded between 2005 and 2006, it finally leaked to the internet in 2012, but fans still consider these gentle folk songs as one of Lana's best-kept secrets.

There was no metadata on the original CD, so some of the track titles were assumed by fans, but the agreed-upon tracklisting is what we've used above.

According to his LinkedIn profile, North Carolina producer Alex Frizzell engineered the album, leading many to assume he handled the production too.

Critical response has been kind, noting Lana's much softer vocals over the simplistic acoustic guitar pluckings, favouring lo-fi ideals rather than the strong electronic pop that later popularised her sound. Her lyrical themes hinted at what was just over the horizon, with a coming-of-age loss of innocence through love and heartbreak.

This tracklisting omits seven songs from her original EPs, namely *For You (From the end.); Wait (From the end.); Blizzard (Young Like Me); You, Mister (Young Like Me); There's Nothing to Be Sorry About (Young Like Me); More Mountains (Young Like Me);* and *In Wendy (Young Like Me).* Two speculated *Sirens* outtakes are *Fordham Road* and *You're Gonna Love Me.* Various other lost tracks are rumoured to be from this era, which is something you have to get used to when studying Lana's discography. As it stands, there are over 200 Del Rey songs that remain unreleased, and those are only the ones we know of. Hard to fathom but impressively true: Lana's unofficial material is more extensive than her official offerings. She has regularly expressed interest in putting together a compilation of her favourite 25 unreleased songs. You can find an up-to-date list of every abandoned tune on Lanapedia here: *https://lanadelrey.fandom.com/wiki/ Category:Unreleased_songs*

# 2.5.
# RELATIONSHIP STATUS: K

An unignorable focal point of *Sirens* is a mysterious, romantic interest anointed with one-letter: *K.* The song
*Drive By* (also known as *For K (Part 1)*) reveals that the man
in question was imprisoned for thirty years and then placed
on death row. Where the line between truth and fiction lies is
anyone's guess, but Lana has confirmed the person's genuine
existence.

Lana lore has run wild with theories connecting the dots
between songs that may or may not be about this figure. Lanapedia lists 26 tracks alone that potentially reference K, with
varying degrees of believability. Most notable is with her later
2012-released track, *Million Dollar Man*, where she opened
up the following backstory:

"It's a song about a man who thought I was one of the most exotic things he had ever seen and me indulging in his appreciation and love. On the outside, he was handsome and wholesome, but under wraps, he was running an illegal electronic business which ended up taking him and his friends under." [25]

# - LANA DEL REY

# 2.6.
# WILLIAMSBURG LIVE SONG-WRITING COMPETITION

In 2006, Lana entered the Williamsburg Live Songwriting Competition under *Lizzy Grant*, the closest Elizabeth would come to using her real name throughout her entire career. She performed some original songs, including one called *Pawn Shop Blues*, which was included on the competition's compilation CD and pushed her to a semi-finalist position. Unfortunately, she did not win, but what she did do was capture the attention of A&R representative Van Wilson who worked for 5 Points Records, owned by David Nichtern. They signed her for a widely-reported $10,000, although the actual amount is under debate.

"It was way more. It was an all-in budget of $50,000. And we also gave her a significant advance. So I'm not sure who's saying what about anything; it seems like people are grabbing at loose facts, but nobody is verifying with anybody." [26]

# - DAVID NICHTERN
(5 POINTS RECORDS OWNER)

# 2.7.
# LIZZY GRANT RECORDINGS

## EP: NO KUNG FU (2006/2007)

1. Brite Lites
2. Get Drunk
3. Jimmy Gnecco
4. Jump
5. Mermaid Motel
6. Put Me in a Movie
7. Yayo

TOTAL RUNTIME: 27:38

With 5 Points Records' support, Lana arranged an un-released demo EP in 2007 titled *No Kung Fu* to drum up interest from producers. It leaked in 2017 with the above tracklist. There is no official cover artwork.

*"I wrote Mermaid Motel because I was so happy. I was on such a roll. I wrote three smashing songs, in my opinion. I wrote Queen of the Gas Station, Jump, and Put Me in a Movie in a week. And that's how it happens. I have to wait so long, I never know how long, could be years [for inspiration], but I know exactly when I have a song, and it comes all at once. It doesn't take long to write. It comes with the melody. It comes with the harmonies and I have to take as long as it takes that day, because then it does leave."* [27]

# - LANA DEL REY

The songs *Get Drunk* and *Jimmy Gnecco* end here with this demo stage (although rumours of their rerecordings do persist) while the others move further with us on our journey.

## MIXTAPE: THE PHENOMENA OF LIZZY GRANT (2005 - 2007)

2. A Star for Nick
*(also featured on Sirens)*
3. Pawn Shop Blues
4. Munny Hunny
5. Rahab II (alternate mix)

TOTAL RUNTIME: 16:22

Curiously, another mixtape may or may not exist from around this time. Reportedly recorded 2005 - 2007, it is known as *The Phenomena of Lizzy Grant*, potentially used for the same producer-hunting purposes as *No Kung Fu*. It was leaked around the end of 2018 with the above tracklist. Again, there is no official artwork to show here.

Ever the giver, *Pawn Shop Blues* was later rerecorded. This goes for *Rahab* too, renamed *For K, Pt. 2* (not to be confused with *Drive By* aka *For K, Pt. 1* on *Sirens*).

## STUDIO 356 SESSIONS (2007)

Around January 2007, six songs were recorded under the Lizzy Grant and the Phenomena moniker and later released on ReverbNation. Tracks included *Disco, Let My Hair Down*, and *Get Drunk* (possibly the same version found on *No Kung Fu*). Additionally, three other songs from these sessions ended up on her *Lizzy Grant aka Lana Del Ray* debut, namely *Oh Say Can You See; For K, Pt. 2;* and *Raise Me Up (Mississippi South)*.

# 2.0.
# RELATIONSHIP STATUS:
# STEVEN MERTENS

At this time, Lana was in a relationship with Steven Mertens, a musician who helped produce many of her early demos, including *Jump*, *Mermaid Motel*, *Put Me in a Movie*, and *Pawn Shop Blues* from the above. There were originally talks of Mertens producing her debut record, but that fell through.

*"I had a seven-year relationship with the head of this label, and he was a huge inspiration to me. I'll tell you later when more people know. He never signed me, but he was like my muse, the love of my life."* [28]

## - LANA DEL REY

The two broke up in 2007, followed by a brief relationship between Lana and producer/guitarist Arthur Lynn.

# 2.9.
# MEET DAVID KAHNE

Using the money from 5 Points Records, Lana moved to a trailer in Manhattan Mobile Home Park, North Bergen, New Jersey.

*"My first record label gave me a small check, and I moved into a park near Manhattan. It's not something I cared to even share, but people keep asking me about it. My songs are cinematic, so they seem to reference a glamorous era or fetishise certain lifestyles, but that's not my aim."* [29]

## – LANA DEL REY

Here, she dedicated herself to songwriting and video making.

*"Our plan was to get it all organised and have a record to go and she'd be touring right after she graduated from college. Like a lot of artists, she morphed. When she first came to us, she was playing plunky little acoustic guitar, [had] sort of straight blonde hair, very cute young woman. A little bit dark, but very intelligent. We heard that. But she very quickly kept evolving."* [30]

## - DAVID NICHTERN

(5 POINTS RECORDS OWNER)

Her demos were sent to famed producer David Kahne, and he agreed to sign her on that very same day. Considering the hit albums under his belt (*Sublime* by Sublime, *Stripped* by Christina Aguilera, and *Rock Steady* by No Doubt, to name a few) and his Grammy Award for Album of the Year 1995 (*MTV Unplugged: Tony Bennett*), there was no doubt that Lana was on a path that could lead her to superstardom.

*"David asked to work with me only a day after he got my demo. He is known as a producer with a lot of integrity and who had an interest in making music that wasn't just pop."* [31]

# - LANA DEL REY

In 2008, Lana graduated with a degree in metaphysical philosophy. At the same time, Lana and Kahne were recording every day, resulting in Lana's first released project:

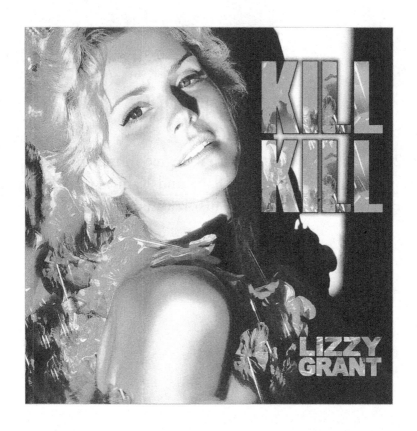

## 2.10.
# EP: KILL KILL (2008)

# KILL KILL (2008)

1. Kill Kill
2. Yayo
*(demo version found on No Kung Fu)*
3. Gramma (Blue Ribbon Sparkler Trailer Heaven)

## TOTAL RUNTIME: 13:34

Under the name Lizzy Grant, the three-track EP *Kill Kill* was released on October 21st, 2008. The album artwork was shot by Lana's sister, Chuck.

*"When I recorded with Davey [David Kahne], we recorded 13 songs. So I was never expecting to release an EP, but when iTunes came to us, and became fervent supporters and said, 'put out anything and we'll give you the artist's spotlight,' we decided, okay, we'll just put out an EP."* [32]

## - LANA DEL REY

All of these songs ended up on her debut.

The opener, *Kill Kill*, was originally titled *The Ocean*,

which Kahne called a "boring" title. Lana crossed it out in frustration and scribbled down *Kill Kill* instead, inadvertently naming the EP in the process. The song was released as a single with a music video featuring shots of Lana wearing an American flag and a Marilyn Monroe hairstyle cut between home video-type clips of California beaches and old cars. Lana would later become famous for this style of video.

*"I once had a boyfriend who talked about all the reasons why he loved flags, Rock-and-Roll, and America. I didn't know much about all of that, but I did love him and I wanted to be just like him. So everything in the videos—the Vegas pyramid, the brides' smile, the groom motioning 'cheers'—they're all different expressions of the happiness I had when I loved a man who loved me and America."* [33]

## - LANA DEL REY

Lana characterised the sound as *"Hawaiian glam metal"*, citing Elvis Presley, Poison, and Van Halen as primary influences. Critical reception was warm, described as lush, cinematic, haunting, soulful, poetic, and elegant (primarily by Index Magazine and The Huffington Post).

# 2.11.
# PRINCESS SUPERSTAR
# SESSIONS

"She was a big fan and wanted to work with me and I wanted to work with her because her voice and style were great." [34]

## - PRINCESS SUPERSTAR

Assumed to be recorded in 2009, Lana worked on some tracks with Princess Superstar, the producer known for her collaborations with Moby, Prodigy, and Grandmaster Flash. None of these songs were officially made public. The four we know about are *Catch and Release, Live Forever, Maha*

*Maha* (aka *Bollywood Hawaii*), and *Moi Je Joue*. These leaked in 2012/2013.

Princess Superstar claims credit for introducing Lana to her future manager, Ben Mawson, but has since had some less-than-kind words about Del Rey's current music.

"It's just too sad and death-oriented and sorry, but I'm about life." [35]

## - PRINCESS SUPERSTAR

## 2.12.
# COMMUNITY SERVICE

E ven though Lana's music career was measurably progressing, her focus at this period was community service, pursuing outreach work for homeless individuals and drug addicts.

*"I'm not a trained social worker. I've been sober for ten years, so it was drug and alcohol rehabilitation. It was more traditional twelve-step call stuff. Just people who can't get it together, me and groups of other*

people who have been based in New York for a long time working with people who need help and reached out. It was about building communities around sobriety and staying clean and stuff like that. That was my focus since I moved to the Bronx when I was eighteen. I liked music, but I considered it to be a luxury. It wasn't my primary focus: the other stuff was really my life. But no one ever... it's not interesting." [36]

# - LANA DEL REY

# PART THREE
# LADIES AND GENTLEMEN, LANA DEL REY

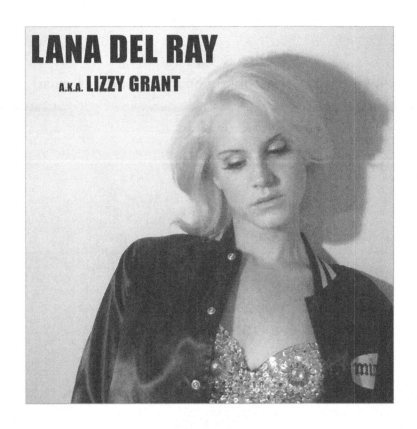

# 3.1.
# ALBUM: LIZZY GRANT
# AKA LANA DEL RAY (2010)

# LIZZY GRANT AKA LANA DEL RAY (2010)

## 1. Kill Kill
*(previously released on the Kill Kill EP)*

## 2. Queen of the Gas Station
*(co-written with David Kahne)*

## 3. Oh Say Can You See

## 4. Gramma (Blue Ribbon Sparkler Trailer Heaven)
*(previously released on the Kill Kill EP, co-written with David Kahne)*

## 5. For K, Pt. 2
*(a reworking of Rahab from The Phenomena of Lizzy Grant)*

## 6. Jump
*(demo found on No Kung Fu)*

## 7. Mermaid Motel
*(demo found on No Kung Fu)*

## 8. Raise Me Up (Mississippi South)

## 9. Pawn Shop Blues
*(demo found on The Phenomena of Lizzy Grant)*

## 10. Brite Lites
*(demo found on No Kung Fu)*

## 11. Put Me in a Movie
*(demo found on No Kung Fu)*

## 12. Smarty
*(co-written with David Kahne)*

## 13. Yayo
*(previously released on the Kill Kill EP, demo found on No Kung Fu)*

## TOTAL RUNTIME: 47:38

*"I want it to sound famous, like a sad party."* [37]

# - LANA DEL REY

The recording of Lana's debut record was reportedly finished in 2008 but was withheld from freedom for two and a half years. It was eventually released on January 4, 2010, titled *Lana Del Ray A.K.A. Lizzy Grant*.

Only *Smarty* and *Gramma (Blue Ribbon Sparkler Trailer Heaven)* had no demo versions because they were written in the studio.

*"Lizzy's Gramma is so important in her life. While we were recording, Lizzy had a picture of her Gramma holding her on her lap. Lizzy was crying and her Gramma has such a sweet smile on her face, in the sun at the beach."* [38]

# - DAVID KAHNE

(PRODUCER; STORY BEHIND THE SONG *GRAMMA*,
QUOTE PREVIOUSLY ON HIS WEBSITE)

Many of these songs came with homemade music videos Lana posted on YouTube. They mostly featured her singing along with her tunes, interwoven with clips she found online. The video for *Jump* features her ex-boyfriend Mike Mizrahi who she dated from 2009 to around 2011.

Critical reception was positive, with Adirondack Daily Enterprise calling it *"eerie"*, *"catchy"*, and *"modern"* while noting its *"Americana themes"*. DN Journal's response was even more glowing, praising its *"hypnotic"* uniqueness, saying its *"inescapable hooks"* will *"stop people in their tracks"*.

*"The album ended up somewhere in between what he (Kahne) wanted and what I wanted."* [38]

## - LANA DEL REY

Something you may have already noticed is that this debut finally boasts the moniker we have come to love: *Lana Del Ray* (although note the slight spelling difference). Lana was evolving, and this release took so long that she had already moved into new realms of artistic identity by the time the world was even invited.

Her name takes inspiration from two different sources. The first was the American pin-up model and film actress Lana Turner, one of the biggest Hollywood stars in the 1940s and 50s. The second was the Ford Del Rey sedan car produced only in Brazil from 1981 to 1991.

*"I wanted a name I could shape the music towards. I was going to Miami*

quite a lot at the time, speaking a lot of Spanish with my friends from Cuba. Lana Del Rey reminded us of the glamour of the seaside. It sounded gorgeous coming off the tip of the tongue." [39]

## - LANA DEL REY

"She was this beautiful young songwriter named Lizzy Grant, it was a cool name. But she wanted to create this thing, Lana Del Rey. We put out the album digitally and at first she wanted it 'R-A-Y' and then we did one version of it that way, and then she wanted to change it to 'R-E-Y' so that was now the third name we were using to promote that artist." [40]

## - DAVID NICHTERN
(5 POINTS RECORDS OWNER)

The title *Lana Del Ray A.K.A. Lizzy Grant* was decided because her former name had been somewhat established, and they were attempting to seamlessly make the changeover to catch up with Lana's ambitions. But in the end, it was too little too late for Lana, and she pulled the album from stores after three months.

# 3.2.
# LANA DEL REY
# BURIES LIZZY GRANT

Shortly after the album's release, Lana met her managers, Ben Mawson and Ed Millett, from Tap Management. With their help, she managed to get out of the contract with 5 Points Records and buy the album rights from them. The album was removed from all digital services before any physical versions were produced.

The reasons for this decision are debated between the involved parties. According to Lana, *"nothing was happening"*.

"*I had signed to an independent label but they couldn't fund the release of it.*" [41]

## - LANA DEL REY

Both Kahne and Nichtern claim that Del Rey simply wanted the record out of circulation because it did not suit the creative direction of where she was headed.

"Her and her new manager came in and said, 'We want to get this off the market. We're going for a completely new deal. We'll buy you out of the deal.' So we made a separation agreement [...] They literally insisted. That's in the contract. We can't have any reference to it anywhere. They were following up on it weekly, 'Oh, there's an obscure website in outer-Mongolia that still has a reference to it, can you tell them to pull it down.' We did. We took it off iTunes and never released it as a hard CD. When I read that it was shelved, that borders on libellous. It's annoying." [42]

# – DAVID NICHTERN

(5 POINTS RECORDS OWNER)

"I think Lizzy Lana owns it, so [her team] wanted it out of circulation. That's why they bought the rights. I think she wanted to be Lana Del Rey and didn't want to be Lizzy Grant. That was her family name, and she's very dramatic. She wiped [out] this other person. I think she actually thinks that she's that other person, and she probably is. So that was the decision that she made, that she didn't want traces of that whole person around, as far as I can tell." [43]

# - DAVID KAHNE
(PRODUCER)

Lana disagreed.

"People act like it's so shrouded in mystery, the 'forgotten terrible album'. But if you look on YouTube, all 13 tracks are available with millions of views, so it's not like no one's heard them. We were all proud of it. It's pretty good." [44]

# - LANA DEL REY

Lana frequently expressed interest in reissuing the album one day, but each year that passes, this idea appears to be more forgotten. If this ever happens, 5 Points Records would see some of that profit.

"We have a deal with her going forward. We don't have ownership or control, but we have participation in that old record. And we have participation in her new records. That's how you do these things [...] we have a participation in her first couple of records going forward as a result of her getting out of her deal. And we still have serious revenue participation if she does anything with her old one." [45]

# - DAVID NICHTERN
## (5 POINTS RECORDS OWNER)

# 3.3.
# LADY GAGA DISS TRACK

While the exact dates are unknown, around 2009 or 2010, Lana recorded a track titled *So Legit*. When it leaked in 2013, everyone quickly connected the dots that the lyrics were against Lady Gaga, including incriminating lines such as:

*"You were the freak King of the*
*piercing shop,*
*All the girls thought they could sing,*
*But they're really not shit,*
*I don't get it,*

You're looking like a man,
you're talking like a baby,
How the fuck is your song in a
Coke commercial? Crazy."

"Stefani, you suck,
I know you're selling twenty million,
Wish they could have seen you when
we booed you off in Williamsburg."

"What happened to Brooklyn?
What happened to our scene, baby?
Have we all gone Gaga crazy?
Remember when the streets used to be
dangerous,
And we were born bad?"

What appears as a result of jealousy in the downtown scene did not have a long-lasting effect, as several photos of the two acting friendly have since spread across the internet.

Lana's response:

"That was a misunderstanding." [46]

# - LANA DEL REY

# 3.4.
# MOVING TO LONDON

With her creative slate wiped clean, Lana moved to London in 2010, living with manager Ben Mawson for a few years. The change of country proved fruitful for her imagination as she wrote around 70 songs while exploring the UK, yet she still found time to visit the USA as often as possible.

*"I've been in London for most of the last two years, but I'll book three months there then go home to New York for three weeks. However, when I'm not working, I go see my friends*

in Glasgow, so I spend my time there when I want to have fun." [47]

## - LANA DEL REY

## 3.5.
# FILM: POOLSIDE

During 2010, Lana (credited as Lizzy Grant) starred in the short film *Poolside*. It was directed by Aaron Peer and shot around New Jersey with a budget of $400. IMDB summarises the plot as *"Ray and JP have a summer job cleaning wealthy people's pools. That is, until Ray gets wrapped up in his strange interest with his patron's personal lives."*

*"[Lana] helped me create her character, notably on the level of diction and performance."* [48]

# - AARON PEER
(DIRECTOR)

When Lana blasted up the fame ladder, interest in the film naturally grew, and *Poolside* was premiered at the 16th Picturestart Film Festival (2012). It won the audience choice award for Best Short Film.

# PART FOUR
# LANA REACHES THE STARS

# 4.1.
# VIDEO GAMES

*"That's five minutes and 20 seconds of ballad. There are no drums in it [...] it feels personal to me, so I wouldn't have thought that that would be the song that people responded to. Although it's a gift for someone like me because, melodically and thematically, it is a perfect representation of me. So it's nice."* [49]

## - LANA DEL REY

In 2011, Lana uploaded two self-made music videos to YouTube. They were for *Blue Jeans* (co-written with Emile Haynie and Dan Heath), and, more importantly, *Video Games* (co-written with Justin Parker). Nothing was the same ever again.

*"I've just been making moving collages online since I was 17. It's just a passion of mine other than singing. Video Games was just one of many, but for some reason—I think because the vocal was so clear—people just really responded to it."* [49]

## - LANA DEL REY

Both videos followed the style of her previous works, combining vintage clips she found online with her face singing the words into her webcam. *Video Games* most notably used paparazzi footage of actress Paz de la Huerta falling when drunk. When Paz was asked what she thought of the video, she responded, *"That's insignificant. I didn't really care."*

Other people cared. That song was an instant winner, spreading around the internet like a sexy virus. The current uploaded official version boasts over 300,000,000 views and counting.

"If I'd known half a million people were going to look at that video, I would've got my hair and make-up done properly. More importantly, I wouldn't have looked so pouty, seeing as everyone talks about my fucking face all the time and sending me awful messages. As much as people seem to like it, I wasn't ready for the personal attacks landing in my inbox." [50]

## - LANA DEL REY

"[I was] trying to look smart and well turned-out, rather than 'sexy'. Of course, I wanted to look good, but 'smart' was the primary focus." [51]

## - LANA DEL REY

A public fascination for Lana was snowballing. Everyone wanted to know who she was and what this song was about.

"A boy. I think we came together because we were both outsiders. It was perfect. But I think with that contentment also comes sadness. There was something heavenly about that life. We'd go to work and he'd play his video games. But also it was maybe too regular. At the time, I was becoming disillusioned with being a singer and was very happy to settle with a boyfriend who I loved. But in the end, we both lost sight of our dreams. Maybe there's something not-so-special about domestic life." [51]

## - LANA DEL REY

# 4.2.
# RELATIONSHIP STATUS: JOSH KEMP

Lana was dating Josh Kemp around from 2010 to 2011, leading most to believe he was the inspiration for *Video Games*. Kemp seemingly confirmed the rumour by posting a live recording of the song to his Insta, captioned with:

*"When your World of Warcraft addiction turns from self deprecating, anti-social depression into iconic and legendary... embrace your darkness...you never know who's watching."* [52]

## - JOSH KEMP

"The verse was about the way things were with one person, and the chorus was the way that I wished things had really been with another person, who I thought about for a long time. That was what happened, you know? He'd come home and I'd see him. But then the chorus wasn't like that. That was the way that I wished it was. The melody sounds so compelling and heavenly because I wanted it to be that way. The verse is more matter-of-fact because that's how it was. It's a mix of memories and the way I wished it could have been." [53]

# - LANA DEL REY

## 4.3.
# VIDEO GAMES RESPONSE

Critical acclaim was unanimous. *Video Games* was dubbed Best New Track by Pitchfork. NME readers ranked it the tenth-best song of 2011. And the love continued until the very end of the 2010s, winning the Q Award for the Song of the Decade while Acclaimed Music ranked it as decade's third-greatest-song based on an aggregation of 35 publications.

*"I learned that there's no reason why people decide they like music when they do. Even if you're the best singer in the world, there's a good chance no one will ever hear you. You make a*

decision to keep singing or to stop. I've been singing in Brooklyn since I was 17, and no one in the industry cared at all. I haven't changed a thing since then, and yet things seem to be turning around for me. Perhaps the angels decided to shine on me for a little while." [54]

# - LANA DEL REY

Such a monumental success brought Stranger Records to the door, quickly signing her up and releasing the song as a single with *Blue Jeans* as the b-side. But with the spotlight came a fiery blast of hate from every angle of the internet.

"People were just so mean to me." [55]

# - LANA DEL REY

# 4.4.
# SUED FOR VIDEO GAMES

One of the first negative repercussions of Lana's sudden attention was due to her careless use of copyrighted material in *Video Games*. She assumed it was royalty free, but it was not, and she was sued for some of the footage.

*"That was a bad day. A million views, and it got wiped out."* [56]

## - LANA DEL REY

The original video was reformatted with new clips to adhere to legal obligations. Thankfully, signing to Stranger Records came with a copyright lawyer to avoid future hiccups.

"So now I have a specialist who reaches out to get permission when I make a video." [57]

# - LANA DEL REY

# 4.5.
# LANA'S AUTHENTICITY

*"Never had a persona. Never needed one. Never will."* [58]

## - LANA DEL REY

As to be expected, the collective keyboard army obsessively dug into Lana's past, uncovering many facts that they could weaponise to discredit the praise she'd only just earned. One of the loudest accusations was one of a fabricated personality, differentiating between the Lizzy Grant and the Lana Del Rey. People questioned her authenticity, calling Lana "manufactured" and a "label-made" personality package. These allegations have been denied by Lana and the entire camp involved.

"My publicists, in their long career, say they have never seen someone be more fictionalised." [59]

# - LANA DEL REY

"It's 2011, it's not like I planned on erasing my history. I've been a pioneer of the internet myself since a decade ago. I was just trying to create something sonically that I could aspire to. First of all, no one was even listening to me for ages, so I did whatever I wanted. I had no fans, the same bands I've talked to for five years, and all of a sudden, everything changed, and they were like, 'You used to be like..' The point is, I know what I like and what to write about thematically, and I have integrity in my musical choices, and I've stuck to that and I think it's a nice gift for me because I have stuck to my guns about what I want to hear sonically, so at least I've done that right. I've made the record I like. I haven't even had that many interviews, so I don't know where they get the stuff they're getting. Not that I'm important or anything, it's just that I don't know. Curiosity is good. That's what [my publicist] Marilyn says." [60]

## - LANA DEL REY

"I'm a lawyer. And if I gave her advice on dressing, it would not be right." [61]

## - BEN MAWSON
(HEAR NO EVIL MANAGEMENT)

"So all along the way, I told her the right way to go, with the name, but she made certain decisions. That's why

I laugh pretty hard when someone said she was put into an image. There's no way you can do that with her. She's very headstrong and knows what she wants." [62]

## - DAVID NICHTERN
### (5 POINTS RECORDS OWNER)

"The vision is all hers." [63]

## - JOHN EHMANN
### (INTERSCOPE RECORDS)

"To be clear, all the detractors saying she's some made-up-by-the-machine pop star are full of shit. While it's impossible to keep the businesses' hands out the pop when creating a pop star, the roots of where this all comes from are firmly inside of Lizzy Grant." [64]

## - TONY "BLOCKHEAD" SIMON
### (FORMER PRODUCER)

"It's not like 1962, where you can't find out about me. My intention was never to transform into a different person. What other people think of me is none of my business. Sometimes, it hurts my feelings. But I have to just keep going. The good stuff is really good. Some of the other stuff is difficult, but I'll be able to tour now, probably sing for a while. That's nice for me." [65]

# - LANA DEL REY

"The name 'Lana Del Rey' was just so I always had a vehicle to be exactly who I was, which is one thing I was upset about that kind of got miscommunicated. [...] I felt free enough to be myself, and that was my way of choosing to do that [...] it doesn't mean I'm in character. It just means I can make art all the time." [66]

## - LANA DEL REY

# 4.6.
# DADDY'S MONEY

Rob Grant's presumed wealth has long haunted Lana's story, but by every account, she did not receive any noteworthy financial support for her career, and despite what the blogs were saying, her contract was not bankrolled by her father.

*"The first time I met or spoke to her father was roughly six months after I signed her, at one of her first shows."* [67]

## - JOHN EHMANN
(INTERSCOPE RECORDS)

*"Her father never had anything to*

do financially with supporting her creativity. I don't know if he was lending her money to live off of, but at least when she was with us, not a penny. I don't know if he's rich or not, I met him and he seemed like a pretty ordinary guy. But that whole thing that she was backed by her millionaire dad is a bunch of crap, basically." [68]

## - DAVID NICHTERN
### (5 POINTS RECORDS OWNER)

Lana has claimed that her father's affluence was always wildly overstated.

"Saying I came from billions of dollars is crazy. We never had any money." [69]

## - LANA DEL REY

# 4.7.
# PLASTIC SURGERY RUMOURS

Forums continue to hypothesise about what work Lana has
done to her face, if anything. Suggestions include lip flip,
lip filler, eyebrow lift with botox, rhinoplasty, jaw contouring
and cheek filler. Lana denies it.

"I haven't had any plastic surgery
done at all. Anyone who's known
me will tell you that. I'm sorry, but I
was living in a trailer park for a
few years. I didn't even have enough
money to buy Cocoa Puffs. It's not like

*I crawled out from under the bridge and got surgery. I'm quite pouty. I'm a pouty person. That's just how I look when I sing."* [70]

## - LANA DEL REY

# 4.8.
# LANA'S TATTOOS

However, Lana is very open about her love for tattoos and is known to have at least 11.

On her right hand, she has the phrases *"trust no one"* and *"die young"*.

On her left hand, there's an *"M"* for her grandmother, Madeleine, and the word *"paradise"* (a theme throughout her work).

On her right arm, she has the surnames *"Nabokov"* (for Vladimir Nabokov) and *"Whitman"* (for Walt Whitman), both writers who have influenced her poetry.

On her left arm, she has *"Chateau Marmont"*, a Los Angeles hotel she references in several songs.

*"It's a place that's inspired so many of my videos and influences a lot of my visuals."* [71]

## - LANA DEL REY

On her chest, she has a list of female names: *"Whitney"* (Houston), *"Amy"* (Winehouse), *"Nina"* (Simone), and *"Billie"* (Holiday).

*"I just like the idea of keeping them close. I like the idea of them coming on tour with me. It makes me happy."* [72]

## - LANA DEL REY

# PART FIVE
# BORN TO DIE ERA

## 5.1.
# EP: LANA DEL REY EP (2012)

## LANA DEL REY EP (2012)

1. Video Games
2. Born to Die
3. Blue Jeans
4. Off to the Races

TOTAL RUNTIME: 17:19

No press is bad press, and Stranger Records signed a joint deal with Interscope and Polydor Records to release Lana's first major label project. It was an EP unimaginatively titled *Lana Del Rey*, which came out on January 10, 2012.

Selling over 24,000 copies in the US, it hit #20 on the US Billboard 200, as well as #6 on both the Billboard Rock Albums and Alternative Albums charts.

Reviews were mixed, primarily because critics called it what it was: merely a promotional teaser for her upcoming album. It's a fair review considering every song here would be featured on that future record.

*"People weren't taking me very seriously, so I lowered my voice, believing that it would help me stand out. Now I sing quite low... well, for a female anyway."* [73]

## - LANA DEL REY

# 5.2.
# THE DISASTROUS
# SATURDAY NIGHT LIVE GIG

Four days after her EP release and Lana was invited to perform on SNL. This fateful show placed Lana under an even bigger spotlight, but for all the wrong reasons.

With a shaky voice and awkward demeanour, she churned through her then-two most popular songs, *Video Games* and *Blue Jeans*. What immediately followed was the harshest of feedback, with Buzzfeed even compiling a list called *"Twenty-six Meanest Quotes from Reviews of Lana Del Rey"*. Some labelled her the worst musical guest in SNL history, and even other celebrities weighed in with their own hate.

"Who is this wack-a-doodle chick performing on 'SNL'? Whaaa?" [74]

## - ELIZA DUSHKU

"Wow, watching this 'singer' on SNL is like watching a 12-year-old in their bedroom when they're pretending to sing and perform #signofourtimes." [75]

# - JULIETTE LEWIS

"Looking back, there was a more eccentric performative approach to it. I was thinking about Maria Callas, or someone darker coming through." [76]

# - LANA DEL REY

Thankfully, other stars rose to her defence.

"It was unfortunate that people seemed to turn on her so quickly. I also think people are making it about things other than the performance. If you read what people are saying about her online, it's all about her past and her family and stuff that's nobody else's business. I don't think [the performance] warranted anywhere near that reaction." [77]

## - DANIEL RADCLIFFE
(THAT NIGHT'S SNL HOST)

"Most people, that would have flattened them forever. It was an outrageous assault [...] I've watched it, and it wasn't that bad." [78]

## - ELTON JOHN

"I'm a good musician. I have been singing for a long time, and I think that [SNL creator] Lorne Michaels knows that. It's not a fluke decision." [79]

## - LANA DEL REY

Three weeks later, SNL addressed the controversy (and largely supported the performance) with a skit where Kristen Wiig played Lana.

"Based on the public's response I must have clubbed a baby seal while singing the Taliban national anthem." [80]

## - KRISTEN WIIG

(AS LANA DEL REY)

"It didn't affect my writing, but it affected my happiness. I became depressed. Because I love New York so much. I was born there, it was my city. I was going to die there." [81]

## - LANA DEL REY

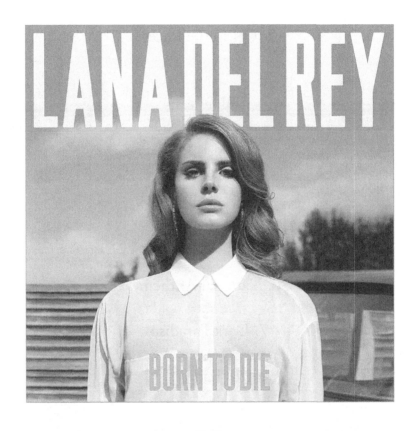

## 5.3.
# ALBUM: BORN TO DIE (2012)

# BORN TO DIE (2012)

## 1. Born to Die
*(co-written with Justin Parker, previously released on the Lana Del Rey EP, second single)*

## 2. Off to the Races
*(co-written with Tim Larcombe, previously released on the Lana Del Rey EP, first promotional single)*

## 3. Blue Jeans
*(co-written with Emile Haynie and Dan Heath, previously released on the Lana Del Rey EP, third single)*

## 4. Video Games
*(co-written with Justin Parker, previously released on the Lana Del Rey EP, first single)*

## 5. Diet Mountain Dew
*(co-written with Mike Daly, demo released in 2010)*

## 6. National Anthem
*(co-written with Justin Parker, The Nexus, and Penny Foster, fourth single)*

## 7. Dark Paradise
*(co-written with Rick Nowels, sixth single)*

## 8. Radio
*(co-written with Justin Parker)*

## 9. Carmen
*(co-written with Justin Parker, second promotional single)*

## 10. Million Dollar Man
*(co-written with Chris Braide)*

## 11. Summertime Sadness
*(co-written with Rick Nowels and Kieran De Jour, fifth single)*

## 12. This Is What Makes Us Girls
*(co-written with Tim Larcombe and Jim Irvin)*

# TOTAL RUNTIME: 49:28

**Bonus tracks:**

13. Without You

*(co-written with Sacha Skarbek)*

14. Lolita

*(co-written with Liam Howe and Hannah Robinson)*

15. Lucky Ones

*(co-written with Rick Nowel)*

Later that month, on January 31, 2012, Lana's major-label debut, *Born to Die* landed through Interscope Records, Polydor Records, and Stranger Records. It was produced by Emile Haynie, famous for his hip-hop work with Eminem and Kanye West. It was recorded in New York City at Electric Lady Studios and The Cutting Room Studios. The cover was shot by Nicole Nodland in Carpenders Park, Watford, UK.

Genre-wise, *Born to Die* has been described with many prefixes to "pop", including alternative, orchestral, baroque, and indie. Some have also noted sadcore and trip-hop influences. Lana's themes of the 1950s/60s Americana and her lyrics about love, sex, and drugs were broadly noted.

*Born to Die* was the fastest-selling album of 2012 and the first to reach 100,000 sold that year. In the US, it shipped 77,000 sales in its first week, debuting at number two on the Billboard 200 (behind only Adele's *21*), eventually becoming the second album (and first debut) by a woman to spend more than 400 weeks in that chart. In the UK, it sold 50,000 copies on its first day and hit number one, while also topping the charts in Australia, France, and Germany. The International Federation of the Phonographic Industry (IFPI) reported it as globally the fifth best-selling album of the year, with sales of 3.4 million copies. Within two years, it had sold seven million copies worldwide, effortlessly certified multi-platinum by the RIAA.

Critical reception was mixed. The Independent on Sunday called it *"a delicious hybrid of Portishead and Nancy Sinatra"*, awarding full marks. Meanwhile, Tiny Mix Tapes scored it an absolute 0, stating, *"I have done my best to place the album, as a series of utterances, in its agony and vacuity"*. The Guardian gave it 4/5 (*"beautifully turned pop music"*). Spin gave it 6/10 (*"Even the terrible parts of Born to Die are just so lovable, which bodes well for the actually great parts"*). Pitchfork gave it 5.5/10 (*"it's the album equivalent of a faked orgasm"*). Rolling Stone gave it 2 (*"pop-trash perversity"*). According to the review-aggregator site Metacritic, this is her lowest-scoring release, with 62.

However, retrospective analysis has been far kinder. Vulture's defence was that it *"came from nowhere with a fully formed aesthetic that was perhaps too much too soon"*. In 2021, Pitchfork sheepishly rescored the album from the former 5.5 up to 7.8.

"I sing low now, but my voice used to be a lot higher. Because of the way I look, I needed something to ground the entire project. Otherwise, I think people would assume I was some airhead singer. Well, I don't think... I know. I've

sung one way, and sung another, and
I've seen what people are drawn to." [82]

# - LANA DEL REY

## BORN TO SINGLES

Video Games was rereleased as the lead single (October 7, 2011). Unable to challenge the viral sensation of the original video, a new one was never filmed. The song reached number one in Germany while hitting the top 10 in Austria, Belgium, France, Ireland, The Netherlands, Switzerland, and the UK. It was called the best song of the year by The Guardian. NME awarded it the 3rd best song of the 2010s, while Pitchfork said it was the 9th.

The lead promotional single, *Off to the Races*, found its way out on December 20, 2011. Some reviewers reacted harshly, called *"a freak show of inappropriate co-dependency"* by NME, while Pitchfork said it *"aim[s] for chatty, sparkling opulence, [but she] doesn't have the personality to bring it off."* The distracting music video consisted of gun-related clips from various films. Idolator fairly observed that *"it seems the video's producer was off to find the cheesiest footage of old shoot-'em-up '80s B-movies for this clip"*. *Carmen* was the second promotional single.

The title track was the second proper single (December 30, 2011). Digital Spy swooned, *"We thought it would be near-impossible for Lana to top the chilling Video Games, but her new* cut—*the title track from her forthcoming album*—*may just have out-haunted its predecessor.*"

With a much bigger budget, Lana finally got her professional music video. It was directed by Yoann Lemoine, known for his work on Katy Perry's *Teenage Dream* and Taylor Swift's *Back to December*. Lana plays "The Lonely Queen" sitting in the French  Palace of Fontainebleau (representing Heaven). Intercut between these are shots of her and her fictional boyfriend (played by model Bradley Soileau). They passionately make out but slowly fall apart, with Soileau holding her bloodied body at the end. The song charted in the top 10 in Denmark, Iceland, Israel, Portugal, Scotland, and the UK.

"The back story. I'm her boyfriend. It's basically like, the boyfriend, you can see the two sides of the relationship where I'm kissing her, then pointing a gun at her head. That's what it is. It's a relationship that is so terrible but neither of them want to leave. That's why when she is in the car, and she wipes the glass, she's looking mad sad, distant, thoughtful. But I'm still trying *to get her attention. That's Kinda the story for it."* [83]

# - BRADLEY SOILEAU

(VIDEO ACTOR)

*Blue Jeans* was the third single (March 30, 2012), which is an interesting choice considering it was already released as a double A-side with *Video Games* and then as the B-side to the *Born to Die* single. Unlike *Video Games*, Lana opted to reshoot this song's video with her newfound resources, this time offering a slo-mo black-and-white affair. Not to mess with the formula, *Born to Die*'s Yoann Lemoine directed this video too, while Bradley Soileau took the main role again, telling the story of two lovers ending in tragedy.

MTV reviewer, Nicole James, was only half-impressed, saying *"While we love LDR's whole 'thing' she has going on, we're wondering when one of her videos is going to have a happy ending. How does she explain fairy tales to the kids she babysits? 'And then Prince Charming kissed Sleeping Beauty and they lived happily ever after... until he got lazy, stopped bathing regularly and became clinically obsessed with World of Warcraft.'"*

The song charted in the top 10 in Belgium, Greece (digital sales), Israel, and Spain. Rolling Stone named it the 35th-best song of the century (thus far, in 2018).

*"I feel like Video Games and Blue Jeans and Born to Die are all like*

*part of a trilogy, I had met this guy and I was really struck by him visually and when it became clear that we couldn't be together anymore, I just knew in my heart that I would still honour that relationship for a long time... It was just more about living in the memories of the best of the past and just honouring that time."* [84]

# - LANA DEL REY

*National Anthem* was the fourth single (June 15, 2012). Directed by Anthony Mandler, the home-videoesque music video saw Lana playing both Marilyn Monroe (performing *Happy Birthday, Mr President*) and Jacqueline Kennedy. Rapper A$AP Rocky played John F. Kennedy in the video, complete with a recreation of the assassination. It was called the 11th best video of the decade by Billboard. Due to its name, the song was watched 58 times more on July 4th, 2017.

*Summertime Sadness* worked as the fifth single (June 22, 2012). Directed by Kyle Newman and Spencer Susser, it stars Newman's wife as Lana's lover, a relationship that ends with both ladies killing themselves. The single charted in the top 10 in Austria, Bulgaria, Germany, Greece, Israel, Italy, Russia, Switzerland, and the US. It landed at number 1 in Poland. In

2013, Cedric Gervais' remix version breathed new life into the song, hitting the top 10 in Australia, Canada, France, Greece, Ireland, and the US. That version also reached number one in Hungary.

The sixth and final single was *Dark Paradise* (March 1, 2013). No music video was released despite Lana announcing one. It reached number 5 in Poland.

## BORN TO DIE UNRELEASED OUTTAKES

*Ghetto Baby* was originally written for *Born to Die* but was given to Cheryl Cole for her third album, 2012's *A Million Lights*. Lana's demo leaked that same year.

*Roses* was recorded in 2011 and leaked in 2016, featuring rapper Theophilus London. A version by Cheryl Cole was also leaked, leading to much speculation that its intended trajectory was the same as *Ghetto Baby*.

*Queen of Disaster* is believed to have been recorded during *Born to Die* sessions. It leaked in 2013 and then blew up as a viral TikTok hit in 2020, garnering millions of views.

Stacks of other known unreleased songs come from this era, such as: *Break My Fall; Damn You; Driving In Cars With Boys; Dum Dum; French Restaurant; Hollywood's Dead; Hundred Dollar Bill; Kinda Outta Luck; Last Girl on Earth; Live or Die; Making Out; Marilyn Monroe/Puppy Love; Meet Me in the Pale Moonlight; On Our Way; Oooh Baby; Paradise* (not to be confused with *Dark Paradise* or the *Paradise EP*); *Prom Song (Gone Wrong); Put the Radio On; Serial Killer; She's Not Me; TV in Black & White; Take Me to Paris; Velvet Crowbar;* and

*You Can Be The Boss.*

All of these can be found online in one form or another, many leaking or posted by Lana herself, sometimes even with her own signature accompanying webcam videos.

"I didn't edit myself [on Born to Die] when I could have, because a lot of it's just the way it was. I was just kinda nervous. I came off sort of nervously, and there was a lot of dualities, a lot of juxtapositions going on that maybe just felt like something was a little off. Maybe the thing that was off was that I needed a little more time or something. Also my path was just so windy to get to having a first record. I feel like I had to figure it out all by myself. Every move was just guesswork." [85]

# - LANA DEL REY

# 5.4.
# MEET RICK NOWELS

In 2011, Lana met hitmaker Rick Nowels, the producer responsible for smash singles from Madonna, Tupac, Celine Dion, Dido, and Stevie Nicks, to name but very few. In a three-day session, Lana and Nowels wrote *Summertime Sadness, Dark Paradise, Lucky Ones*, and *TV in Black & White*, the first three of which made the debut record. Since then, Lana has kept Rick extremely busy, the man credited on every album from here to 2021's *Blue Banisters*.

*"One of the reasons why I like Rick so much is because a lot of producers, when they get in the studio with an artist, they want to challenge them*

or they want to break them down to build them back up again. I just find that really unhelpful. But Rick always says yes, and he's really fluid. If I'm stuck with an idea lyrically and I just want to say 'screw it' and move on, he doesn't really care; we just move on to a new idea. So he's very easy, and he contributes a lot. He plays almost everything, all the keyboard parts, all the guitar, so he's pretty amazing." [86]

# - LANA DEL REY

## 5.5.
# BORN TO DIE INSPIRATIONS

*"I was a big drinker at the time. I would drink every day. I would drink alone. I thought the whole concept was so fucking cool. A great deal of what I wrote on Born To Die is about these wilderness years. A lot of the time when I write about the person that I love, I feel like I'm writing about New York. And when I write about the thing that I've lost I feel like I'm*

*writing about alcohol because that was the first love of my life. Sure, there have been people, but it's really alcohol."* [87]

## - LANA DEL REY

Throughout her career, Lana has worn her influences on her sleeve, coming not only from musicians and iconic figures, but events in her own life, including friends, lovers, and locations.

*"I had a vision of making my life a work of art, and I was looking for people who also felt that way."* [88]

## - LANA DEL REY

Musically, Lana has named the following artists as inspirations: Amy Winehouse, Andrew Lloyd Webber, Beach Boys, Billie Holiday, Bob Dylan, Bobby Vinton, Britney Spears, Bruce Springsteen, Cat Power, Courtney Love, The Crystals, The Eagles, Eminem, Frank Sinatra, Joan Baez, Julee Cruise, Julie London, Leonard Cohen, Lou Reed, Miles Davis, Nina Simone, and Nirvana.

Lana has mentioned Elvis Presley as an influence more often than most of the above. In 2008 (under the alias Sparkle

Jump Rope Queen), she recorded a song titled *Elvis*, which was later given to Eugene Jarecki for his 2017 *The King* documentary.

"I knew Elvis' songs would be the soundtrack to my life as soon as I laid eyes on his photograph. I know when I love something as soon as I see it." [89]

# - LANA DEL REY

"I think one thing that really affected me was when I was 11. I saw Kurt Cobain singing Heart-Shaped Box on MTV. I saw the video for it. That was something that really struck me when I was younger." [90]

# - LANA DEL REY

She has also noted the soundtrack to *American Beauty* as a direct inspiration for *Born to Die*.

"I have artists who have influenced me a lot, but I don't think you would naturally find them as comparisons to me." [88]

# - LANA DEL REY

"I would have loved to be part of the indie community. But I wasn't. I was looking for a community, I don't even know any people who are musicians. I never met that popular indie, whoever the fuck that is. Who IS indie? First of all, I can't really get my head around what indie music is. Because if you've heard of it, it's sort of pop music, right? Because it's, like, popular? Or is it just that it's not on the radio? It's not like I was in an indie community and then I blew up. It's like, I was living on the street and

*I'm not [popular]. You know what I'm saying?"* [91]

## - LANA DEL REY

Outside of music, Lana's songwriting would not be the same without Walt Whitman and Allen Ginsberg. Furthermore, the film work by David Lynch and Federico Fellini, the painting work by Mark Ryden and Pablo Picasso, and the presence of acting star Lauren Bacall made a substantial difference.

*"The funny thing is that my style is something that no one ever asked me about until a couple of years ago. For years it was all music-driven. I really loved Nina Simone, Kurt Cobain was my driving influence, I listen to everything Bob Dylan did [...] but in terms of actual female style icons? No. I was impressed with what someone like Karl Lagerfeld built and did and the house that he made. But there was never really a female figure I wanted to emulate [...]*

A lot of the reason my look is the way it is, is because it's really easy to put on a sundress every night if I have to perform—or just wear jeans every day and a flannel or something. Stylistically, I love make-up. I love doing my own make-up and stuff, but clothes-wise, I actually didn't ever really care. Initially the fashion world was more interested [in me] than the music world, which was strange when I first started singing [...] I don't actually care. But because of the way I look, it looks like I really do care." [92]

# - LANA DEL REY

"Image is important but I'm a writer first. I've been a writer since I was very young and I'm a singer second.

Then, you know, the editing and the visuals and the photographs and the movies. Those come after." [93]

# - LANA DEL REY

## 5.6.
# RELATIONSHIP STATUS: BARRIE-JAMES O'NEILL

Another impossible-to-miss inspiration is the boys in Lana's life.

*"I just wondered why we were here and was sort of consumed by the fact that everyone was gonna leave this planet. When I fell in love for the first time, it was just really inspirational. It's a good mix knowing that you're going to die but also being*

excited by true love with fleeting
moments of happiness." [94]

## - LANA DEL REY

As Lana was zooming into fame in 2011, she met Scottish singer-songwriter Barrie-James O'Neill. Their relationship was confirmed in 2012, and the two had a very creative partnership, with O'Neill co-writing many of her later songs.

"I think there's more than one for everybody. I could meet one person, but like other people too. I've seen it happen before: people who have their true loves, with many great loves around them." [95]

## - LANA DEL REY

"I never thought I'd have the luxury of loving someone and being loved. But when it happened, it really was what they talked about in the movies." [96]

## - LANA DEL REY

Engagement rumours thrived when the two were spotted house-hunting in 2013 while Lana wore a suspicious-looking ring. This was never confirmed, and the couple called it quits after three years in 2014.

"You should honour love, even when it's lost. I've been separated from various things and people in my life that I wanted to stay close to. By staying calm and being strong, I was honouring the memory of those things and those people. I'm proud of that, and I continue to do that." [97]

## - LANA DEL REY

# 5.7.
# TOUR: BORN TO DIE TOUR

L ana has often spoken about her stage fright and dislike of live shows. When she saw the hologram of Tupac at the Coachella festival, she half-joked to her manager, *"Right there is the future of my live tours."*

*"I'm not a natural performer but my fans know that. I think if you go to see the show, you go because you want to be there not just because you're going to watch and see if I'll mess up and die."* [98]

## - LANA DEL REY

Regardless, on November 4, 2011, Lana embarked on her first worldwide concert tour. With only four dates in small venues, the demand shouted for something larger, encouraging Lana to add more dates at bigger venues. The tour started in Manchester and moved across the UK and Europe while also landing in Canada, the States, and Australia (39 in total). Her show in Japan was cancelled due to exhaustion.

"It was daunting. I love to sing and I really love to write, but in terms of being onstage, I'm not that comfortable, which I think is sort of clear. Um, so. I don't remember what you said." [99]

## - LANA DEL REY

# PART SIX
# PARADISE ERA

## 6.1.
# HIRED GUN

With great fame comes great opportunity. Legendary soul artist Bobby Womack released his 27th album, *The Bravest Man in the Universe*, on June 12, 2012 (his first in 12 years). Lana was featured on the *Dayglo Reflection* song. Sadly, this was Womack's final offering, as he passed two years later.

In September 2012, the Paris Motor Show invited Lana to be the face of the Jaguar F-Type. This car was later featured in her promotional short film for the song *Burning Desire*, released on 2013's Valentine's Day.

*"The allure of Jaguar is in large part due to its duality. It has a unique blend of authenticity and modernity,*

which are two values we believe are shared with Lana in her professional achievements." [100]

## - ADRIAN HALLMARK
(JAGUAR'S GLOBAL BRAND DIRECTOR)

"Making art means making tough decisions. I do believe you create your own life path and that you will be rewarded for following your passions, and sticking to it. It's just good to know now, with people like Jaguar and working with them, that I'm not the only one out there with such strident, creative beliefs." [101]

## - LANA DEL REY

In that same month, Lana covered Bernie Wayne and Lee Morris' song *Blue Velvet*. A video was released for the H&M 2012 autumn campaign, where Del Rey is an Americana lounge singer in front of a small room of people. It was directed by Johan Renck and drew comparisons to David Lynch's film of the same name. A behind-the-scenes video was posted to H&M's channel, and Lana modelled for the company too.

## 6.2.
# FILM: RIDE

*"I always write the concepts for the videos [...] I always make a visual mood board. I use iMovie and I take clips of everything else, and I usually map it out from one second to four minutes."* [102]

## - LANA DEL REY

Still hanging out in September 2012, it was on the 25th that Lana released *Ride*, the first single from her upcoming EP, *Paradise*. Produced by the legend Rick Rubin, it was originally a demo which Lana refused to let go.

"I loved this demo I did with Justin Parker, who I wrote a lot of things with like Video Games, Born to Die, and National Anthem. Ferdy Unger-Hamilton at EMI hated the song. So I think him and Rick [Rubin] had been talking and Rick was like, 'What's going on with Lana? Can she come over, I hear she's in L.A'. I think I had been over to say 'Hi' to him first. Just to say 'Hi'. We took a walk in Santa Monica—he takes the same walking route every morning. Then, a few weeks later, I brought him Ride, and he really liked it [...] Working with him was good. I was still in my old car, my old Mercedes that was barely making it that hour-and-a-half drive down to Shangri-La Studios in Malibu, and it was really good. He has this sprawling lawn with *all these bunnies and palm trees. He was very relaxed."* [103]

# - LANA DEL REY

*Ride* received mass critical love, cementing her reputation as an artist with far more to give past her debut. MTV called it the number one Must Hear song of the week. Complex named it the eighth-best song of 2012. It reached the top 10 in Belgium and Russia.

*"After years of staying true to my own artistic visions, I met Anthony Mandler, who shared my love of all things dark and beautiful and understood my passion and reverie for the country that America used to be. He's helped me to bring the visions of my imagination to life and tell my different life stories through film."* [104]

# - LANA DEL REY

Soon following was the epic 10+ min short film *Ride*, directed by Anthony Mandler and premiering at the Aero Theatre in October. The response was far less warm, owed entirely to the themes presented. It's unsurprising, due to Lana portrayed as a sex worker making her rounds in a biker gang, and while many praised her acting, they were put off by what they considered anti-feminist and a romanticisation of prostitution. Lana was also seen holding a gun to her temple while wearing a Native American headdress, leading to further upset about pro-suicide ideas and cultural appropriation.

"Yeah. Like, I remember it was the San Francisco Chronicle or whatever who wrote this huge thing about me being an anti-feminist. But the thing is, I don't really have any commentary on the female's role in society. It was the same with my first song that got big, Video Games. People had criticisms about it being submissive and whatever, but nothing I ever wrote had a message. It was just my own personal experience, and it's the same with Ride. I believe in free love and that's just how I feel. It's just my experience of being with different

Kinds of men and being born without a preference for a certain type of person. For me, that is my story in finding love in lots of different people, and that's been the second biggest influence in my music." [105]

# - LANA DEL REY

# 6.3.
# LANA'S ANTI-FEMINISM

Segueing neatly into the next pile of Lana backlash, another public fury that tormented her career was anti-feminist accusations. This opposition took a more fierce flight due to her *Ride* video. Lana has said much on the topic.

*"To be honest, I don't really have [a take on feminism]. I have a great appreciation for our world's history. I learn from my own mistakes, I learn from the mistakes we've made as a human race. But I think we've gotten to a good place as women and we'll*

just keep naturally progressing. That's kind of how I feel about it." [106]

## - LANA DEL REY

"For me, the issue of feminism is just not an interesting concept. I'm more interested in, you know, SpaceX and Tesla, what's going to happen with our intergalactic possibilities. Whenever people bring up feminism, I'm like, god. I'm just not really that interested." [107]

## - LANA DEL REY

"A true feminist is someone who is a woman who does exactly what she wants. If my choice is to, I don't know, be with a lot of men, or if I enjoy a really physical relationship, I don't think that's necessarily being anti-feminist. For me, the argument of feminism never really should have come into the picture. Because I don't know too much about the history of feminism, and so I'm not really a relevant person to bring into the conversation. Everything I was writing was so autobiographical, it could really only be a personal analysis." [108]

## - LANA DEL REY

Even back around the *Video Games* era, she faced conflict about her lyrical choices.

"People talk about me being an anti-feminist because of that song. They think it's coming from a place of submissiveness. But in reality, it was more about coming together and doing your own things happily in the same living space." [109]

## - LANA DEL REY

As the years rolled on, Lana took on a more active stance. She identified herself as a  third-wave feminist and supported the #MeToo movement.

"Because things have shifted cultur-ally. It's more appropriate now than under the Obama administration, where at least everyone I knew felt safe. It was a good time. We were on the up-and-up. Women started to feel less safe under [the Trump] admin-istration instantly. What if they take away Planned Parenthood? What if we can't get birth control? Now, when people ask me those questions, I feel a little differently." [110]

# - LANA DEL REY

Lana revisited the topic in 2020 with a lengthy Instagram post. Here are some snippets:

"I just want to say it's been a long 10 years of bullshit reviews up until recently, and I've learned a lot from them. But also, I feel it really paved the way for other women to stop 'putting on a happy face' and to just be able to say whatever the hell they wanted in their music. Let this be clear, I'm not not a feminist—but there has to be a place in feminism for women who look and act like me—the kind of woman who says 'no' but men hear 'yes'—the kind of women who are slated mercilessly for being their authentic, delicate selves—the kind of women who get their own stories and voices taken away from them by stronger women or by men who hate women." [111]

# - LANA DEL REY

# 6.4.
# AMERICAN POLITICS FEAT.
# TRUMP AND KANYE WEST

In a political conversation, one could be forgiven for assuming Lana as an excessively patriotic nationalist due to her constant references to America in her work. However, her relationship with her country is far more intricate.

*"I'd be lying if I said I didn't love any fucking film or book that wasn't based around the underbelly of society. I've always loved that. But on the other hand, I'm kind of simple in the way that I love the movement of a super-eight flag waving in the*

wind. The same with the palm trees and that sepia colour of the fifties film. Like a lot of my choices had to do with the grade of the film. It was that simple, purely aesthetic. Same with my interest in photographers and things like that. A lot of it is just the look of it. I just like it." [112]

## - LANA DEL REY

"I was happy for the American people because [Obama] was a symbol that they needed to feel better [...] I have a lot of political opinions [...] I get a lot of grief for just talking about my own musical choices. I don't usually talk about my views these days that much on politics." [113]

## - LANA DEL REY

"It's complicated because everything has changed for me. Before I had no money. And now everything I make, I lose. So I don't have money again, because I lose half. Healthcare reform—that needed to be addressed. I still don't have health insurance because I haven't been back to the United States since the time when I couldn't afford healthcare because it was seven hundred dollars a month." [114]

# - LANA DEL REY

Del Rey has regularly come out swinging against former US President Donald Trump. During Trump's first year of presidency, Del Rey claimed she tried to use witchcraft against him. She was particularly vocal after the 2021 January 6 Capitol attack.

"Trump is so significantly impaired that he may not know what he was doing due to his significant lack of empathy. The wider-ranging problem is the issue of sociopathy and narcissism in America." [115]

# - LANA DEL REY

"The madness of Trump... as bad as it was, it really needed to happen. We really needed a reflection of our world's greatest problem, which is not climate change but sociopathy and narcissism. Especially in America. It's going to kill the world. It's not capitalism, it's narcissism." [116]

# - LANA DEL REY

"We didn't know that we got half of the country who wants to shoot up the Capitol. We didn't really know that because we never got to see it. I think this gave us the opportunity to

see where our level of mental
health is at." [117]

# - LANA DEL REY

After her extensive vocal opposition against Trump, Lana was relieved when Biden became the 46th President of the United States. Inspired by his 2020 acceptance speech, Lana released a cover of *On Eagles' Wings*, a devotional hymn originally by Michael Joncas.

"Again, not that I believe it's anyone's business at all, but I made it clear who I voted for." [118]

# - LANA DEL REY

Like many people, Lana also became critical of Kanye West during his support of Trump with a lengthy comment beneath one of his Instagram posts.

"I can only assume you relate to his personality on some level. Delusions of grandeur, extreme issues with narcissism. None of which would be a talking point if we weren't speaking about the man leading our country. If you think it's alright to support someone who believes it's OK to grab a woman just because he's famous, then you need an intervention just as much as he does." [119]

## - LANA DEL REY
(ADDRESSING KANYE WEST ON INSTAGRAM)

"Kanye West is blond and gone." [119]

## - LANA DEL REY
(LYRICS FROM *THE GREATEST*)

It's worth mentioning that Kanye and Lana were former buddies. In May 2014, Lana performed at Kanye West and Kim Kardashian's wedding rehearsal dinner at the Palace of Versailles. Rumours claim she made $3 million for the gig, but Lana denied this, stating she would *"never charge her friends"*.

"It was beautiful. I'm a huge fan of Kanye's, he's so talented. I'm genuinely happy for them that they've found something so amazing in their union. When Kanye wanted me to come and sing and surprise Kim, I definitely wanted to be there. So we flew from the AMFAR reception at Cannes to Versailles and it was pretty much what you expected. It's Versailles!" [120]

# - LANA DEL REY

(LYRICS FROM *THE GREATEST*)

# 6.5.
# VEGETARIANISM

While details are hazy, it is widely reported that Lana has been a vegetarian since perhaps 2006.

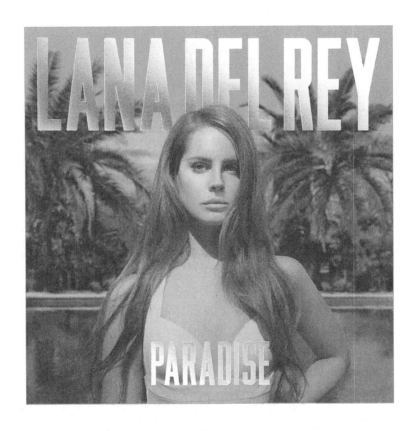

## 6.6.
# EP: PARADISE (2012)

# PARADISE (2012)

## 1. Ride
*(only single, co-written with Justin Parker)*

## 2. American
*(co-written with Rick Nowels and Emile Haynie)*

## 3. Cola
*(co-written with Rick Nowels)*

## 4. Body Electric
*(co-written with Rick Nowels, later featured in Tropico)*

## 5. Blue Velvet
*(Lee Morris and Bernie Wayne cover, previously released as a promotional single for the H&M campaign)*

## 6. Gods & Monsters
*(co-written with Tim Larcombe, later featured in Tropico)*

## 7. Yayo
*(previously released on the Kill Kill EP and Lizzy Grant aka Lana Del Ray debut, demo found on No Kung Fu)*

## 8. Bel Air
*(co-written with Dan Heath, later featured in Tropico)*

## TOTAL RUNTIME: 34:03

### Bonus tracks:
## 9. Burning Desire
*(co-written with Justin Parker, previously released for the Jaguar campaign, only available on the iTunes edition of Paradise)*

"[I was] in a better mood, staying in one place in California. It was kind of a summing-up of the idea of living at the Chateau Marmont—and then I moved out. It was kind of a closing door. I like that it feels more lush and tropical, and I like that it has more of a Pacific Coast sound at times, like Gods & Monsters. Paradise is my favourite record, I love it." [121]

# - LANA DEL REY

Lana's third EP, *Paradise*, was released on November 9, 2012, through Polydor and Interscope. Most tracks were produced by Rick Nowels, but there were contributions from Justin Parker, Dan Heath and *Born to Die*'s Emile Haynie. It was recorded between London (Electric Lemon Studios SARM Studios, The Square Recording Studio), Malibu (Shangri La Studios), Santa Monica (The Green Building), and Los Angeles (Westlake Studios). The cover art was shot by Nicole Nodland (the same photographer for *Born to Die*), snapped on the set of the *Blue Jeans* video.

"I only worked with [Rick Rubin] for six days, because he only worked on Ride. But I worked with the same guys I worked with for Born To Die. I've only ever worked with those guys. Emile Haynie, he comes in at the end, and then there's Rick Nowels and Justin Parker who write the music underneath the songs. I write the words and melody, and they write all the chords and music. And then Dan Heath comes in for the string arrangements, after which Emile puts in the beats and soundscaping, like birds and bells." [122]

# - LANA DEL REY

The EP was also repackaged and released as one with the debut, known as *Born to Die - The Paradise Edition.*

"I think it's like a less specific version of the last record in a lot of ways.

*I like it more because I did it really easily and it just feels a little more raw to me. I got to record most of it in Santa Monica, so kind of has more of a West Coast Pacific Blue sound. There's just a lot more electric guitars. Not in a rock way, just in a kind of beachy way."* [123]

# - LANA DEL REY

*Paradise* sold 67,000 in its first week in the US, debuting at number 10 and eventually selling over 332,000 units there. It also hit 10 in Canada.

The response was ever-so-slightly warmer than what *Born To Die* unfairly received. With an 8/10, Drowned In Sound thought that the *"music here is more considered and richly teased out"*. Tiny Mix Tapes (who had famously slapped *Born to Die* with a 0/10) admitted that *"Paradise is the best attempt (yet) to cohere a deeply incoherent artist"*, giving it a 5/10. Slant Magazine offered it a 6/10 but labelled the record a *"grubby cash grab"*, especially considering how close to Christmas time it was released. According to the aggregate site Metacritic, it was rated 64 overall, a whopping 2% higher than *Born to Die*.

Regardless, people were starting to take notice, and this record was nominated for Best Pop Vocal Album at the 56th

Annual Grammy Awards (losing to *Unorthodox Jukebox* by Bruno Mars). She won a 2012 MTV Europe Music Award for Best Alternative performer, the Brit Award for International Female Solo Artist, and two Echo Awards for Best International Newcomer and Best International Pop/Rock Artist.

## OTHER NOTEWORTHY SONGS FROM PARADISE

B esides the aforementioned *Ride, Blue Velvet,* and *Burning Desire,* several other *Paradise* tracks are worth discussing.

Cola was set to be the second single, but that never materialised. Still, the song managed to cause quite a fuss. For starters, its opening lyric, *"My Pussy Tastes Like Pepsi Cola"*, definitely raised some eyebrows.

"My boyfriend [Barrie-James ONeill] is Scottish. He deems American girls very exotic. He once told me: 'You American girls walk around as if your pussies tasted like Pepsi-Cola, as if you'd wrap yourself into an American flag to sleep.' He deems us all very patriotic." [124]

## - LANA DEL REY

The lyric *"Harvey's in the sky with diamonds, and he's making me crazy"* was called to attention when many assumed it was referencing disgraced film-producing sex offender, Harvey Weinstein. Del Rey confessed she had a character based *"on both him and Harry Winston"* in mind. She dropped the song from her live sets after the sexual harassment charges surfaced, stating she now finds the track *"uncomfortable"*.

The song *Yayo's* inclusion was particularly notable, as it was first found way back in 2007 on the *No Kung Fu* demo collection. It was later re-recorded, the same version found on both the *Kill Kill* EP and the *Lizzy Grant aka Lana Del Ray* debut. The third and final version is found here, making it the only song from Del Rey's first studio album to get such an official treatment.

A promotional video for *Bel Air* was released in November 2012, made entirely out of unused footage from the *Summertime Sadness* shoot. Curiously, the video was made private in February 2013.

## PARADISE UNRELEASED OUTTAKES

*Young and Beautiful* was constantly teased by Lana in interviews (sometimes under the title *Will You Still Love Me*); hence fans were surprised when it didn't show up on the tracklisting. The song eventually settled on the *Great Gatsby* soundtrack.

A song called *Hollywood* was rumoured to have been recorded for *Paradise*. It leaked in 2013, but Lana asserts this version had the incorrect instrumental. She expressed her desire to release the proper mix herself one day.

"When you let everything go, all these little things come to you when you aren't expecting them to. I was writing a song that seemed a little left-of-centre and too specific to be used for anything. And then this guy was looking for something with a theme that was exactly what I had just written. It was called Life Is Still Beautiful, so it was about a guy and his best friend, and one guy is just trying to get his best friend to come back to him because life is still beautiful." [125]

# - LANA DEL REY

*Life Is Beautiful* was written for *Paradise*, but when a producer for *The Age of Adaline* film requested a song, Lana reworked this tune for them. The track was featured in promotional videos for the movie (released in 2015) but was never officially released. In 2020, two versions of the song leaked.

*I Don't Wanna Go* was recorded for *Paradise*, but didn't make the cut. Lana tried again, later re-recording the song for *Ultraviolence* (then known as *Lake Placid*), but like before, it was not deemed appropriate for that release either.

Other speculated songs from this era are *Wild One, I Talk to Jesus, JFK,* and *Starry Eyed.* However, due to the close recording dates, some of these may have been intended for *Ultraviolence.*

# 6.7.
# TOUR: PARADISE TOUR

On April 3, 2013, the 93-show *Paradise Tour* kicked off, starting in France, crossing all over the UK, the EU, the Nordics, South America, and North America, as well as playing shows in Lebanon, Russia, and Turkey. This included a stop at the 2014 Coachella Valley Music and Arts Festival. Eighteen months later, it concluded on October 18, 2014, at the Hollywood Forever Cemetery in Los Angeles. Due to the 2014 Gaza War, her show in Israel was cancelled.

The 18 tracks used to aid the videographer leaked on October 15, 2020.

# 6.0.
# COVERS AND SOUNDTRACKS

During this period, Lana found time to release cover songs while contributing to assorted film soundtracks, often with a video kindly included.

The first was her take on Leonard Cohen's *Chelsea Hotel#2* (March 28, 2013), featuring Lana singing with a series of close-ups of her face while cigarette smoke flickered in moody lighting. Cohen's original was about a romantic encounter with Janis Joplin at the Hotel Chelsea in New York City. On November 6, 2017, Lana performed the song with Leonard's son, Adam Cohen, for the *Tower of Song: A Memorial Tribute to Leonard Cohen* concert.

The second cover was Lee Hazlewood and Nancy Sinatra's *Summer Wine* (April 19, 2013), where Lana shared vocal duties with then-boyfriend Barrie-James O'Neill, both appearing in the home video-styled music video. The original was a b-side to Nancy's most famous song, *Sugar Town.*

*"There's a movie coming out this summer that's set in the 1920s, and it's been fun for me to write love songs for the woman."* [126]

# - LANA DEL REY

As previously mentioned, *Young and Beautiful* was recorded for *Paradise* but reworked for the 2013 adaptation of *The Great Gatsby*, starring Leonardo DiCaprio, Tobey Maguire, and Carey Mulligan. The song was co-written with Rick Nowels and released as a buzz single on April 23, 2013. It debuted at number 89 on the United States Billboard Hot 100 (her highest yet). The song peaked at number 22, while hitting the top ten in Australia, Israel, Greece, Hungary, Ukraine, and Italy. It was nominated for Best Song Written for Visual Media at the 56th Annual Grammy Awards but lost to Adele's *Skyfall*. However, it did win Best Original Song at the 18th Satellite Awards.

The reception was positive, with critics using various favourable terms to describe the track, including *"haunting"*, *"typically lush"*, *"classy"*, and *"silky"*. Fuse remarked, *"if the single takes off, perhaps the songbird can finally scrub her image clean of that 'Girl that totally f-cked [sic] up her Saturday Night Live debut' tag."*

Another *Young and Beautiful* arrangement, known as *Dan Heath's Orchestral version*, was also put together and was used as the audio for the official music video. Here, Del Rey sings in a dark room with glittery diamond tears on her cheek, supported by a full-string orchestra.

Lana's soundtrack work kept marching on. Angelina Jolie handpicked Lana to cover the 1959 *Sleeping Beauty* song *Once Upon a Dream* (written by Jack Lawrence and Sammy Fain) for the *Maleficent* film. Released on January 26, 2014, critics were impressed, calling it *"moody and low-key"* (Forbes), *"swoony and spaced-out"* (Stereogum), as well as *"much darker"* (Hypable) and *"sombre and sinister"* (Complex) when compared to the original.

On December 23, 2014, Lana contributed two originals to Tim Burton's biographical drama film *Big Eyes*, about the life of painter Margaret Keane. The first took its name from the film and was co-written by Dan Heath. It was nominated for Best Original Song at the 72nd Golden Globe Awards but lost to *Glory* by Common and John Legend (for the film *Selma*). It was also shortlisted as a potential nominee for the Best Original Song Oscar but did not make it that far. The second *Big Eyes* tune was called *I Can Fly*, originally meant for *Ultraviolence* and co-written with Rick Nowels.

*"Tim showed her the film and she fell in love with it [...] Women in particular seem to get the movie, and Lana really got the movie. The whole thing is about a woman who can't find her voice. It almost becomes a*

musical. Lana's song expresses what Margaret is feeling so perfectly, it's like a soliloquy of her inner thoughts." [127]

# - LARRY KARASZEWSKI
(BIG EYES PRODUCER/COWRITER)

# 6.9.
# LEAKS AND RETIREMENT

*"Oh, I don't think I'll write another record. What would I say? I feel like everything I wanted to say, I've already said."* [128]

## - LANA DEL REY

Much to her fans' horror, Lana perpetually alluded to her uncertainty around making another album, citing things like fame as causing a block in her creativity.

"*I don't think [fame has] been conducive to writing, being on the road and all that. I don't really feel inspired to write at all, but beforehand, when I was in Brooklyn for nine years... I was kind of a night owl and just walked around and met weird people. That was me picking up life experiences and meshing them into my own. That really did it for me... I really feel like I need six months to live again. Time to be normal or abnormal. I don't have anyone writing anything for me. It's such an internal well, and if it's not full, it's just not full.*" [129]

## - LANA DEL REY

When Clash Music asked whether she ever thought about quitting music, she responded, *"every day"*.

"I didn't want to do it, ever. You can make music just for making music. You don't have to put it on YouTube, and that was definitely a viable option for me. I have a lot of passions and making music was always something I would do for fun. However, from what happened, it wasn't worth it most of the time." [130]

# - LANA DEL REY

"When people ask me about it, I just have to be honest. I really don't know. I don't want to say, 'Yeah, definitely— the next one's better than this one,' because I don't really hear a next one. My muse is very fickle. She only comes to me sometimes, which is annoying." [131]

# - LANA DEL REY

Another devastating blow to her progress came when some-one hacked one of her hard drives and leaked a slew of unre-leased songs, the most concerning track called *Black Beauty*, for which Lana had big plans (and was eventually released as a bonus song on *Ultraviolence*).

"Somebody remotely accessed my hard drive, so even songs I've never emailed to myself [were accessed]. There are hundreds of them." [132]

## - LANA DEL REY

"I do feel discouraged, yeah. I don't really Know what to put on the record. But I guess I could just put them on and see what happens." [133]

## - LANA DEL REY

Rumours of Lana's separation from the music world reached culmination when she announced her *Tropico* short film by calling it *"the farewell project"* on Twitter.

# 6.10.
# FILM: TROPICO

On December 4, 2013, Lana premiered the surreal musical short film *Tropico* at the Cinerama Dome, Hollywood. Directed by Anthony Mandler, it visually reinterprets three of her songs from the *Paradise EP* into Biblical stories.

*"When I was studying philosophy, my teacher told me that it's okay to feel like the people you're closest to aren't alive anymore. Sometimes that is the best company to keep. It's about the people that pondered the same questions as you did, and*

had the same sort of life mentality as you. I was upset and inspired by that premise. I knew then, really, that my closest friends would be people I have never really met before. I was different and I didn't know many people who felt about mortality how I did. As a result, I do feel a personal connection with the icons: John Wayne, Elvis. I loved how nice Marilyn was, I related to her. Finding girls who were as loving and warm as her is hard." [134]

# - LANA DEL REY

## TROPICO CHAPTER 1 – BODY ELECTRIC

Lana plays Eve in the Garden of Eden. Adam (played by Shaun Ross), Jesus, Marilyn Monroe, and Elvis Presley are all there. God is a John Wayne character. Eve eats the apple from the Tree of Knowledge and then faints. Adam eats the apple too, and the two are cast out of Paradise.

## TROPICO CHAPTER 2 – GODS & MONSTERS

A modern-day Adam and Eve are now living in Los Angeles. Eve (Lana) is a stripper, while Adam is a gang member. Walt

Whitman's *I Sing the Body Electric* and Allen Ginsberg's *Howl* are recited by Del Rey. Adam and his gang rob a party of wealthy men.

## TROPICO CHAPTER 3 – BEL AIR

God narrates John Mitchum's poem *Why I Love America*. Adam and Eve drive to the countryside and are baptised. The two ascend back into heaven on flying saucers.

The *Tropico EP* (featuring the above songs plus the video) was released on December 6, 2013.

The reception was mixed to positive, with many taking issue with the nonsensical narrative but praising the arty imagery. Regardless, fans were relieved during the premier when Lana announced that she was no longer retiring and was wrapping up a new record.

*"I really just wanted us all to be together so I could try and visually close out my chapter before I release the new record, Ultraviolence."* [135]

# - LANA DEL REY

# PART SEVEN
# ULTRAVIOLENCE ERA

# 7.1.
# ALBUM: ULTRAVIOLENCE (2014)

# ULTRAVIOLENCE (2014)

## 1. Cruel World
*(co-written with Blake Stranathan)*
## 2. Ultraviolence
*(co-written with Daniel Heath, third single)*
## 3. Shades of Cool
*(co-written with Rick Nowels, second single)*
## 4. Brooklyn Baby
*(co-written with Barrie O'Neill, fourth single)*
## 5. West Coast
*(co-written with Rick Nowels, first single)*
## 6. Sad Girl
*(co-written with Rick Nowels)*
## 7. Pretty When You Cry
*(co-written with Blake Stranathan)*
## 8. Money Power Glory
*(co-written with Greg Kurstin)*
## 9. Fucked My Way Up to the Top
*(co-written with Daniel Heath)*
## 10. Old Money
*(co-written with Daniel Heath and Robbie Fitzsimmons)*
## 11. The Other Woman
*(Nina Simone/Jessie Mae Robinson cover)*

## TOTAL RUNTIME: 51:24

**Bonus tracks:**
## 12. Black Beauty
*(co-written with Rick Nowels, formerly leaked)*

13. Guns and Roses
*(co-written with Rick Nowels)*
14. Florida Kilos
*(co-written with Dan Auerbach and Harmony Korine)*
15. Is This Happiness
*(co-written with Rick Nowels; iTunes Store bonus track)*
16. Flipside
*(co-written with Blake Stranathan;*
*Target & Fnac special edition bonus track)*

*"It is absolutely gorgeous. Darker than the first. So dark it's almost unlistenable and wrong. But I love it."* [136]

# - LANA DEL REY

Early 2014, Lana's third studio album, *Ultraviolence*, was already completed with Rick Nowels in Electric Lady Studios, New York. However, upon meeting Dan Auerbach, Lana decided to rerecord the album with him behind the wheel. On June 13, 2014, it was released on Interscope/Polydor Records. Largely a production collaboration between herself and Dan, it also featured contributions from Blake Stranathan, Daniel Heath, Barrie O'Neill, Greg Kurstin, and (of course) Rick Nowels. It was mostly recorded in Auerbach's studio in Nashville (Easy Eye Sound) but also around California (The Bridge in Glendal, Echo in Los Angeles, The Green Building in Santa Monica) and London (The Church). The cover artwork was shot by Neil Krug, setting off a long artistic relationship between the two. The title is a common phrase from Anthony Burgess' 1962 novella/Stanley Kubrick's 1971 film *A Clockwork Orange*, but Lana has distanced herself from the reference.

"I found the title before I had written almost any of the songs that are on it now. I love the idea of having a one-word title because I think that has a beautiful simplicity. I was thinking of flowers at the time, and since I love flowers that are shades of blue and violet, I had this idea of ultraviolet and that kind of vibration. That was the basis for the title and of course it became more suggestive. Ultra is a sweet sound and completely opposite to the sense of violence. It also summarises some of the contradictions I find in myself; that my essence is sweet but I also have this violence in my life that I've experienced over the last four year." [137]

## - LANA DEL REY

Most likely owed to Auerbach's ear, *Ultraviolence* was a different sound for Lana, incorporating dream pop, psychedelic rock, and desert rock with some soft blues and indie.

"When I met Dan, something that he really tapped into was that all of my choruses slipped into half-time beats and half-time swings. He called it 'Narco Swing' every time the West Coast chorus would kick in and that's a good description of it. It has a late-seventies feel but there's also a nod to the West Coast nineties synth sound that comes in." [138]

## - LANA DEL REY

With upwards sales of 182,000, *Ultraviolence* debuted at number one on the Billboard 200, Lana's first to do so. It held the record for most album sales by a female artist for most of 2014, until Taylor Swift overtook it in November with *1989*. It's the eighth best-selling 2014 vinyl in the US. It also hit number 1 in Australia, Belgium, Canada, Denmark, Finland, New Zealand, Norway, Poland, Scotland, Spain, and the UK. It sold over a million copies worldwide within a month of release.

*"It's a little more stripped down but still cinematic and dark."* [139]

# - LANA DEL REY

Critical acclaim was immediate. Consequence and Entertainment Weekly each awarded it full marks, with the latter stating, *"Ultraviolence is the masked bacchanalia that finally unleashes the full potential lurking beneath the hype"* and that *"Kubrick would have loved Del Rey—a highly stylised vixen who romanticises fatalism to near-pornographic levels, creating fantastically decadent moments of film-noir melodrama. It's an aesthetic that demands total commitment from both artist and listener, and it would be difficult to buy into if she didn't deliver such fully realised cinema"*. Many directly declared it as a superior project to *Born to Die*, such as Sputnikmusic (*"It's the very definition of a grower, and this record has something Born to Die never had: more reflection."* - 86 score) and Billboard (*"Auerbach offers a more sedate take on the Born to Die template, lightening the orchestrations, ditching the hip-hop beats, and presenting Lana as a perpetually scorned pop-noir fugitive [...] It's a delicious contrast that makes for a surprisingly great album."* - 83 score). There were many 80s (Q Magazine, Spin

Magazine, NOW Magazine, Fact Magazine, All Music, Pop Matters, DIY Magazine, and The Guardian) and a stream of 70s too (No Ripcord, Rolling Stone, musicOMH.com, Drowned in Sound, Exclaim, Clash Music, and Slant Magazine).

Lana was finally winning the media over, but not everyone was on board just yet. There was a 60 from NME (*"The line between self-aware irony and tragically conforming to type is thin, though, her knowing winks getting stuck in a tangle of false eyelashes, and ultimately undermining what had the potential to be a powerful artistic statement."*). There was a 50 from Chicago Tribune (*"Ultraviolence almost qualifies as a parody. Unfortunately, there's not enough punch in the songs to make listeners care whether she's joking or not."*). And there was a low 30 from The 405 (*"In her grand tradition of coining absurd descriptive phrases, Del Rey and Auerbach have christened all this 'narco swing', an apt characterisation if only one assumes it's short for narcoleptic; it takes some doing to make sex, drugs, and rock'n'roll sound boring, but in her hands, the vices of hedonism scan as crushingly monotonous."*). The record ultimately scored a 74 on the aggregator site Metacritic.

Regardless, the end-of-year accolades spoke volumes, sitting in the top 10 albums of 2014 according to The Boston Globe (1), Slant Magazine (3), Rolling Stone (pop genre, 3), Entertainment Weekly (4), NPR (4), Spin (pop genre, 5), Time (5), and Juice Nothing (7). Fast-forward to the end of the decade, and it was ranked the 25th Best Pop Album by Consequence, the 11th Best Album by Cracked, and the 44th Best Album by Juice Nothing.

## ULTRAVIOLENCE SINGLES

"When I played [the label] West Coast, they were really not happy that it slipped into an even slower BPM for the chorus. They were like: 'None of these songs are good for radio and now you're slowing them down when they should be speeded up'. But for me, my life was feeling murky, and that sense of disconnectedness from the streets is part of that." [140]

# - LANA DEL REY

*West Coast* was introduced to the world when Lana performed it at Coachella Music Festival on April 13, 2014. The next day, it was released as the lead single. Critics adored the song, responding well to its rhythmical shift as if two songs in one. It was described as *"revolutionary"* (Muu-Muse), *"silky-smooth"* (Nylon), and *"darkly surfy and dripping in femme fatale"* (Oyster). Many publications recognised *West Coast* as one of the best songs of the year, ranked number 3 by both Cosmopolitan and Music Times, 11 by NME, and 25 by Consequence. The Huffington Post accurately observed that *West Coast* was *"perhaps too dark to win the song of the summer title it deserved"*. The single debuted at number 17 on the Billboard Hot 100, her highest yet, while also reaching the top 10 in Belgium (4), Greece (3), and Israel (5).

"That's what someone just said to me when I was on the beach, I was at a beach party, he said 'they've got a sayin' if you're not drinking, then you're not playing'. I thought it was a cute opening line. For me, it's like thinking about the way things were for me, and how my motivations were for so long. They still seem a part of my life even though I'm not drinking now. For some reason I really like soaking up the mood of a really dynamic party whether it's on the West Coast or whatever. I like that other people can have fun and let loose. I feel like I'm a part of it when I'm there." [141]

# - LANA DEL REY

(DISCUSSING *WEST COAST*'S OPENING LYRIC)

The Vincent Haycock-directed music video was released on May 7, 2014. It was shot in black-and-white around Marina del Rey and Venice, Los Angeles, where Lana is torn between two "bad boy" love interests, including Hollywood tattoo artist Mark Mahoney (famous for inking the likes of Rihanna, Jared Leto, Lady Gaga, and Marilyn Manson). It was nominated for the 2014 MTV Best Cinematography Video Music Award but lost to Beyoncé's *Pretty Hurts*.

"Meeting some people like Mark Mahoney, who's an amazing tattoo artist. He's done a lot of my tattoos, and he did the early 90s rapper's tattoos, like on Biggie and Tupac. He's been through so much, just this effortlessly cool character, and has such a history in his face and in his attitude. There's so many characters in California." [142]

# - LANA DEL REY

*Shades of Cool* was the second single (or first promotional single), released May 26, 2014. Again, critics were impressed, many placing it in a cinematic context, with Slate claiming it would *"fit perfectly in a James Bond theme track"* while Rolling Stone suffixed that notion with, *"directed by Quentin Tarantino"*. PopMatters stated that *"Del Rey has never sounded better"*. It peaked at 79 on the US Billboard Hot 100 while charting well in Greece (3) and Hungary (19).

Jake Nava directed the video, which was released on June 17, 2014. Like *West Coast*, it starred Mark Mahoney as Lana's love interest, but unlike *West Coast*, it is a far brighter and more colourful piece. That said, an alternate version does exist where she drowns in the end. Classic Lana.

The *Ultraviolence* title track was the third single, released on June 4, 2014. Sadly, its reputation was damaged by controversy, most notably for its glorification of domestic violence with the line *"he hit me and it felt like a kiss"* (which itself was taken from the 1962 single of that name by the Crystals).

*"This sort of shirt-tugging, desperate, don't leave me stuff. That's not a good thing for young girls, even young people, to hear."* [143]

# - LORDE

Lana has since refused to sing that line live.

*"I don't like it. I don't. I don't sing it. I sing Ultraviolence but I don't sing*

that line anymore. Having someone be aggressive in a relationship was the only relationship I knew. I'm not going to say that that [lyric] was 100 percent true, but I do feel comfortable saying what I was used to was a difficult, tumultuous relationship, and it wasn't because of me. It didn't come from my end." [144]

# - LANA DEL REY

A music video was released on July 30, 2014. The entire clip was shot on an iPhone using the 8mm Vintage Camera app. The location was Portofino, Italy, where Lana is wearing a wedding dress and walking into the Cappella di San Sebastiano church. It was directed by Francesco Carrozzini, who Lana started dating soon after. Interestingly enough, another video was shot for the *Ultraviolence* song but was scrapped for reasons unknown. That footage was eventually used in the *Honeymoon Sampler*, as well as her music videos for *Music to Watch Boys To* and *Freak*.

*Brooklyn Baby* was released on June 8, 2014, as the fourth single. Focusing on New York hipster culture, Del Rey wrote the song with Lou Reed on her mind, even referencing the late singer with the line *"And my boyfriend's in a band, he plays guitar while I sing Lou Reed"*. Lana had planned to work with Reed, but he died the day she arrived to do so.

"*I took the red eye, touched down at 7am, and two minutes later, he died.*" [145]

# - LANA DEL REY

The song was treasured by critics, The Fader calling it *"the standout track of Ultraviolence"*, while Rolling Stone said it was *"dreamy"* before placing it as number 22 on their 50 Best Songs of 2014 list. The song hit number 6 in Finland and 10 in Russia. No music video was released.

Despite the aforementioned leaky drama, the bonus track *Black Beauty* was eventually released on January 5, 2013 as the final single. MuuMuse called it *"one of Lana's greatest epics"*.

## OTHER NOTEWORTHY SONGS FROM ULTRAVIOLENCE

*Sad Girl* went viral on TikTok in late 2022 with hundreds of thousands of videos using it, millions of views following. Rolling Stone called it *"the most alluring ballad"* on the record.

"*Sad girl, 'cause I'm still sometimes a sad girl, still things beyond my control.*

Sometimes I do things that I want, above what I maybe should do." [146]

# - LANA DEL REY

*Pretty When You Cry* appeared to have come close as a single release when Lana previewed a music video on Instagram, but it was never released or leaked.

"The way you heard it recorded is the way I freestyled it. I made it up on the spot with my guitar player and left it as it was with that session drummer, and just called it a day on that song. Like the vocal inflexion has its own narrative, it's not all lyric drive, it's just kind of moments in time that are meaningful to me, left as they were, kind of untouched. The fact that I didn't go back and try to sing it better is really the story of that song, because that's sort of me revealing to you a facet of myself. I *don't care that it's not perfect. That's why that song is more important in that way than what I'm actually saying."* [147]

# - LANA DEL REY

*The Other Woman* is best known as a Nina Simone favourite, featuring on her albums *Nina Simone at Carnegie Hall* (1963), *Let It All Out* (1966), and *Live at Ronnie Scott's* (1984). It was written by Jessie Mae Robinson. Lana's variation also went viral on TikTok in early 2022 with millions of views.

The bonus track *Guns and Roses* is of particular interest due to fiery rumours of a whirlwind romance between our girl and GnR lead-singer, Axl Rose, when they were spotted together at Chateau Marmont in West Hollywood. To fuel the flames, Rey wore a Guns N' Roses t-shirt at a Camden Jazz Café concert several days later. Lana has always been very eager with her admiration for the man, including penning a song for him way back in 2008 called *Axl Rose Husband* (under her moniker Sparkle Jump Rope Queen). Nobody knows the full story, but ex-guitarist DJ Ashba rejected the relationship idea.

*"I don't think they're dating. Axl is a really cool dude and he likes to hang out with cool people."* [148]

## - DJ ASHBA
(EX-GUNS N' ROSES GUITARIST)

And, of course, we have *Fucked My Way Up to the Top*, the hard-hitting title which inspired the name for the very book you're reading.

*"People have offered me opportunities in exchange for sleeping with them. But it's not 1952 anymore. Sleeping with the boss doesn't get you anywhere at all these days. Nobody cared about wanting to change the way I looked or sounded because no one was interested in the music."* [149]

## - LANA DEL REY

# ULTRAVIOLENCE UNRELEASED OUTTAKES

In 2013, fruitful sessions with Rick Nowels produced *I Can Fly*, *Yes to Heaven*, *Shades of Cool*, *Sad Girl*, *Is This Happiness* and *Your Girl*. Three of these were cut.

An unedited mix of *Fine China* was leaked in 2017. A later version was considered for *Blue Banisters*.

*Yes to Heaven* was later rerecorded for *Honeymoon* and *Lust for Life* but was scrapped each time. There are reportedly over 100 mixes of the song. Many versions have leaked.

*Your Girl* has never fully leaked, but due to various stems and snippets, fans and professionals alike have put together their own versions.

*Queen of Hearts* was written in the earliest sessions for *Ultraviolence*, and Mike Will Made It produced the demo. The song finally leaked in 2022. Another Mike Will Made It collaboration named *Don't Stop* is rumoured to come from these sessions.

*Wait for Life* was written with Emile Haynie during *Ultraviolence* sessions, but Haynie used the song for his record *We Fall* in 2015. Reaction was positive.

*Cherry Blossom*, *Nectar of the Gods*, *Living Legend*, and *If You Lie Down with Me* were penned for *Ultraviolence* but were cut only to be reused later on *Blue Banisters*.

Other songs include *Angels Forever, Forever Angels*; *Cult Leader*; *Dragonslayer*; *Hollywood*; *JFK*; *Starry Eyed*; *Unidentified Flying Bill*; *Ave Maria*; and *I Talk to Jesus*. Many of these have leaked at least in part. Due to the close recording dates, some of these may have been intended for the *Paradise EP*.

# 7.2.
# MEET DAN AUERBACH

"And then, on the last night, I met Dan. We went out to a club, we looked at each other and we were like, 'Maybe we should do this together?' It was rare for me, because it was really spontaneous. Five days later, I flew to Nashville and played all our tracks to Dan. We had been talking about this 'tropiCali' vibe, about how I loved LA, and that *it was grounding me. I felt like the energy in LA was really sexy. But being there also enhanced my love for the East Coast, in being away from it. We really had this West Coast sound in mind, but with an East Coast flavour. And then we recorded it in the middle of the country. It was an American amalgamation."* [150]

## - LANA DEL REY

When Lana met Dan Auerbach of Black Keys, something clicked in her creative head. Apparently, Lana felt there had been a lack of fuzzy guitar tone on her records, to which Auerbach responded, *"Well, I'm pretty known for the fuzz."* Lana liked that and thought, *"Maybe this is my guy!"*

*"Trying to write things that I thought would be more accessible. It's this feeling that comes over you, like falling in love. You have to get that sensation."* [151]

## - LANA DEL REY

# 7.3.
# RELATIONSHIP STATUS: FRANCESCO CARROZZINI

As noted above, Italian photographer Francesco Carrozzini directed Lana's video for the *Ultraviolence* title track. The two began dating soon afterwards, around June 2014. The relationship was creative, with Carrozzini directing her *Honeymoon* video in 2015, but they split after just over a year, in November 2015.

# 7.4.
# MARILYN MANSON RAPE VIDEO

In November 2014, a video titled *Sturmgruppe 2013 Reel* was uploaded to (and quickly removed from) YouTube. Set to an ambient drone song, a slow-motion shot of Marilyn Manson surrounded by girls suddenly cuts to Lana Del Rey acting out a scene where Eli Roth rapes her (Eli being the horror director famous for *Hostel* and the *Death Wish* remake).

*"The footage is so sick, it's been locked in a vault for over a year."* [152]

## - ELI ROTH

This led people to believe it was a Marilyn Manson music video, which he denied, claiming the Lana footage and his footage were filmed separately but later spliced together.

*"It wasn't a Marilyn Manson video. The editor of the company that put it out was somebody who's edited my videos, that video was something that was done with a camera that Eli [Roth], who's my friend, and I both wanted to test out, so I let him test it out."* [153]

## - MARILYN MANSON

*"Eli and I wanted to do a music video with her, but she was being such a problem. Although I still respect her, I'm friends with her. I just left, I was tired, I was not willing to make that part of the video. Eli and I originally had intentions of making a video with her, but that is not the intention that is represented in that film clip*

*because that is not what I filmed, not for my video."* [154]

# - MARILYN MANSON

Everyone appears to have distanced themselves so far from the project that it is confusing to calculate any exact truths behind the details. Meanwhile, Lana has never even acknowledged the scene's existence.

# 7.5.
# TOUR: THE ENDLESS SUMMER TOUR

Lana's third headlining concert tour began on May 7, 2015, to support the *Ultraviolence* album. Almost every show sold out instantly. Most of the gigs were supported by Grimes, except for seven of them that Courtney Love opened. Courtney has expressed her desire to work with Lana in the future.

*"I have a distinctive voice and it might sound cool if it's the right song."* [155]

## - COURTNEY LOVE

The tour only covered the USA and Canada with 20 shows over two months, grossing $6 million.

# 7.6.
# SUICIDE AND THE LOVE-COBAIN FAMILY

Lana's admiration for Nirvana is public knowledge and was already covered earlier in this book. But the ties to that family run deeper than just fan adoration, with Courtney Love regularly gushing Lana many compliments to her face.

*"What I hear in your music is that you've created a world, you've created a persona, and you've created this kind of enigma that I never created but if I could go back I would create."* [156]

## - COURTNEY LOVE

However, their dynamic was not always a walk in the P-A-R-K tonight. In a 2014 interview, Lana typically romanticised death by musing about joining the infamous 27 Club, a collection of legendary musicians who died at that age, including Robert Johnson, Rolling Stones' Brian Jones, Jimi Hendrix, Janis Joplin, Jim Morrison, Amy Winehouse, and of course, Kurt Cobain.

*"I wish I was dead already. I don't want to have to keep doing this. But I am."* [157]

# - LANA DEL REY

Kurt and Courntey's daughter, Frances Bean Cobain, was not impressed, taking to Twitter to @Lana.

*"[Lana], the death of young musicians isn't something to romanticise. I'll never know my father because he died young & it becomes a desirable feat because ppl like u think it's 'cool'. Well, it's f---ing not. Embrace life, because u only get one life. The ppl u mentioned wasted that life. Don't be I*

*of those ppl...ur too talented to waste it away."* [158]

## - FRANCES BEAN COBAIN

Frances later clarified:

*"I'm not attacking anyone. I have no animosity towards Lana. I was just trying to put things in perspective from personal experience."* [159]

## - FRANCES BEAN COBAIN

Lana suggested she had been misquoted, and that the interviewer was asking leading questions.

*"I want to stay hopeful, even though I get scared about why we're even alive at all."* [160]

## - LANA DEL REY

# PART EIGHT
# HONEYMOON ERA

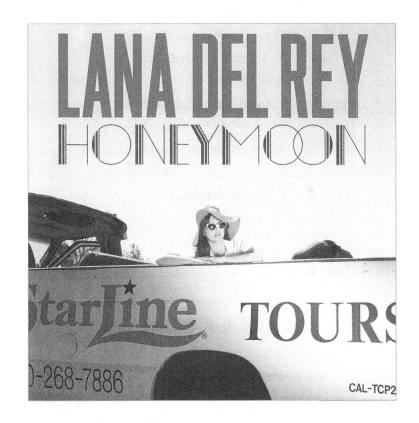

# 8.1.
# ALBUM: HONEYMOON (2015)

# HONEYMOON (2015)

## 1. Honeymoon
*(co-written with Rick Nowels, promotional single)*

## 2. Music to Watch Boys To
*(co-written with Rick Nowels, second single)*

## 3. Terrence Loves You
*(co-written with Rick Nowels, promotional single)*

## 4. God Knows I Tried
*(co-written with Rick Nowels)*

## 5. High by the Beach
*(co-written with Rick Nowels and Kieron Menzies, first single)*

## 6. Freak
*(co-written with Rick Nowels)*

## 7. Art Deco
*(co-written with Rick Nowels)*

## 8. Burnt Norton
*(Interlude, written by T. S. Eliot)*

## 9. Religion
*(co-written with Rick Nowels)*

## 10. Salvatore
*(co-written with Rick Nowels)*

## 11. The Blackest Day
*(co-written with Rick Nowels)*

## 12. 24
*(co-written with Rick Nowels)*

## 13. Swan Song
*(co-written with Rick Nowels)*

## 14. Don't Let Me Be Misunderstood

*(Nina Simone cover, written by Sol Marcus, Bennie Benjamin and Gloria Caldwell)*

## TOTAL RUNTIME: 65:06

*"It's a vibe record. Obviously I love playing with words and they're important to me, but sometimes the soundscaping or the sonic atmospheres are just as important. I had more fun being playful with the production on this record than I did on some of the other ones."* [161]

# - LANA DEL REY

Wasting no time, Lana zipped back into the studio and had her fourth studio album ready for release by September 18, 2015, through Interscope and Polydor.

*"I love the word 'honeymoon' and I guess I just loved the idea of hoping that everything's gonna turn out really*

beautifully. It's probably the most romantic word out there." [162]

## - LANA DEL REY

It was recorded in The Green Building (Santa Monica, California) and Electric Lady Studios (New York City) with longtime producers Rick Nowels and Kieron Menzies. Sessions with production juggernaut Mark Ronson took place, but no fruit was harvested from them.

"I hate to crap all over your excitement, but we just worked a couple days together and I think she's amazing, but we didn't actually end up doing anything for her album. I shouldn't have opened my big mouth, but I love that track Honeymoon and the stuff I've heard from the record is great." [163]

## - MARK RONSON

The cover artwork was shot by her sister, Chuck Grant. The image featured a 1-800 phone number which fans called, some lucky enough to speak to Lana Del Rey herself.

Unlike her last three releases, *Honeymoon* did not come with any deluxe or special editions. Lana's promotion was unique, relying on a short trailer, radio interviews, music videos, fan meets, and social media. On release day, Mel's Drive-In on Sunset Blvd. offered promotional "Honeymoon" milkshakes.

*"The narrative for this record was kind of a tribute to LA, I guess, because of the soundscaping that we had. Like a lot of amazing strings. I feel the mood was the narrative, but it's a lot of descriptive pieces about driving at night or being in love or not being in love. Kind of the same old thing."* [164]

# - LANA DEL REY

Reversing from the grungy guitar-driven sounds of *Ultraviolence*, Lana returned to the retro ambient trip-hop baroque pop of her earlier work with some slow jazzy undertones thrown in for good measure. Lyrically, she continued her obsession with romance, lust, drugs, violence, and, of course, the American way.

With 116,000 sales, *Honeymoon* debuted at number two on the US Billboard 200. In Australia, she hit number one, her third consecutive album to do so. The record also hit the top 10 in Austria (4), Belgium (2), Canada (3), the Czech Republic (6), Denmark (7), The Netherlands (5), France (3), Germany (4), Greece (1), Ireland (1), Italy (2), Mexico (2), New Zealand (2), Norway (6), Poland (3), Portugal (2), Scotland (2) Spain (4), Sweden (3), Switzerland (3), and the UK (2).

Much like *Ultraviolence*, the critics were on board with *Honeymoon*. Particularly glowing reviews came from Drowned In Sound (*"You've [Lana Del Rey] found your own style and run with it. It's amazing to see someone so free and in control."*) with a 90 score; The Guardian (*"With a little chopped-and-screwed modernity, hints of jazz and Morricone-like soundscapes, there's a timelessness to Honeymoon, and an intrigue that should linger longer than her previous LPs."*) with an 80; and Pitchfork (*"Honeymoon just synthesises ideas she's been vamping on from the beginning into a unified work. She figured where she was going long before she got there; with Honeymoon she has finally arrived."*), with 75. Less enthusiastic reviews came from The Quietus (*"Del Rey plays a winning strike with Honeymoon's four opening songs: powerful ballads, lain on ethereal and soft arrangements made of smooth strings and jazzy winds... if High By The Beach still can sustain its four-minutes length, the same unfortunately cannot be said for the most of the following songs"*) with a 50 score; Pretty Much Amazing (*"Del Rey has struggled to back up her provocations with substance. Ultraviolence was an exception, a singular breakthrough. Honeymoon is, sadly, a slip and fall after a promising stride forward."*) with a 58; and Slant Magazine (*"It's a full hour of expressively expressive-less music—unmitigated solipsism as an aesthetic choice."*) with 60. Regardless, its Metacritic aggregated score totalled 78, beating

*Ultraviolence* by 4%. That said, Metacritic's 8.6 fan score was 0.2 lower than *Ultraviolence*.

Come the year end, NME called it the 7th Best Album of 2015, The New York Times called it the 9th, and Rolling Stone dubbed it the 2nd Best Pop Album of the Year.

## HONEYMOON SINGLES

*H*igh by the Beach was the first single, dropping on August 10, 2015, to immense acclaim. Most publications called attention to its mass market appeal, called *"radio-friendly"* (Billboard), *"Del Rey's catchiest"* (Entertainment Weekly), and *"far more commercially minded"* (State). Its summer vibes were also widely praised, with *"Lana's knack for capturing summer in songs is on point here"* (MTV News) and that Lana *"knows how to do summer right"* (HitFix). Naturally, the drug connotation did not go unnoticed, Out Magazine dubbing the song a *"new 420 anthem"* while State again observed that *"if it wasn't for that title and the heavy drug references, we'd imagine this would fit quite snuggly on the charts and radio rotation"*. Some end-of-year lists called it the 75th (Pitchfork) and 18th (Rolling Stone) best song of the year.

An error with Nielsen's calculations claimed the single debuted at number 7, when it was much lower, at 51. It also charted at number 4 in Israel and 1 in Sweden.

The Jake Nava-directed music video arrived on August 13, 2015. An obvious commentary on her fame, a hand-held camera follows Lana around her beach house while a paparazzi helicopter pesters her. In response, Lana retrieves a large firearm and blasts the helicopter into debris. Both Pitchfork and Time Magazine called it the 10th-best video of the year.

*"I started to think about this idea for High by the Beach, which Kind of had a similar theme of being afraid that you were being watched while you were at home. So I guess there's like a small sense of glamorised paranoia."* [165]

# - LANA DEL REY

*Terrence Loves You* was the first promotional single, released on August 21, 2015. Some fans who phoned the *Honeymoon Hotline* on the album cover were treated to this song's premiere. This lyrics reference David Bowie's hit *Spacy Oddity* with the line *"Ground control to Major Tom"*. Del Rey has dubbed *Terrence Loves You* as her favourite song from the record because *"it's jazzy"*.

The *Honeymoon* title track was the second promotional single, released on September 7, 2015, to critical adoration. NME claimed it as *"perhaps her most heart-stopping ballad yet"*, while Billboard said it was *"grander and more ambitious than anything the singer-songwriter has released thus far"*.

*"[The song Honeymoon is] where the record begins and ends [...] it*

encapsulates all of the things that come naturally to me." [166]

# - LANA DEL REY

A lyric video was uploaded to YouTube on July 14, 2015. Lana directed and edited an official music video herself, but it remained unreleased for some time.

"You haven't seen the full video for Honeymoon because I didn't put it out yet. I don't know if I will because I made it myself [...] nothing really happened in it." [167]

# - LANA DEL REY

The video leaked in 2016, and Lana did ultimately host it on her channel too. Shot in VHS, it primarily featured close-ups of Lana's face and her going for a stroll.

*Music to Watch Boys To* was the second single, released on September 11, 2015. It was initially announced as a possible album title.

"I have this idea for this record called Music to Watch Boys To, so, yeah, I'm just Kind of thinking about that and what that would mean." [168]

## - LANA DEL REY

"The title lends itself to a visual of shadows of men passing by, this girl's eyes, her face. I can definitely see things." [169]

## - LANA DEL REY

Critics were happy enough with the track, although some took issue with its slow pacing. It hit number 17 on the Sweden Heatseeker charts.

The official music video premiered on September 30, 2015. Shot around Hollywood, California, here we see Lana lounging in a lawn chair and girls swimming in their underwear while the boys play basketball and skateboard.

## OTHER NOTEWORTHY SONGS FROM HONEYMOON

Despite not being released as a single, *Freak* was honoured with an epic 10-minute music video using snippets from unused *Ultraviolence* clips. The first portion features Father John Misty as a cult leader, while the second half employs much of the same footage from *Music to Watch Boys To* with the girls swimming in their underwear set to Claude Debussy's poem

*Clair de Lune.* Much of these visuals were also seen in the *Honeymoon Sampler,* dropped onto YouTube on September 8, 2015.

"I really love Rae Sremmurd, so that might be a surprise inspiration. Also, Sage The Gemini. I really love listening to some of the people that came out of Atlanta in the last two years. I don't think I was trying to emulate that sound, but I had elements of it in Freak and High By The Beach." [170]

# - LANA DEL REY

*Burnt Norton* was premiered to fans calling the *Honeymoon Hotline* from the artwork. The track is an interlude where Lana recites lines from T. S. Eliot's poem *Burnt Norton*, first published in his *Collected Poems 1909–1935* (1936).

"I originally wasn't going to use that little excerpt, but I was looking up poems about time and timelessness, and he has that line about the still point of the turning world, where

everything was real. I loved that
because I feel so often I'm trying to get
everything to just feel like it's moving
and to feel new. But I always feel
really caught up in it. A real stillness.
And I always wonder if that's what
it feels like in the great
beyond whatever." [171]

# - LANA DEL REY

*Salvatore* may feature lyrics that sound like they were written by ChatGPT in the style of Lana Del Rey (*"Ah ah ah ah, ah ah ah ah, cacciatore. La da da da da, la da da da da, limousines. Ah ah ah ah, h ah ah ah, ciao amore. La da da da da, la da da da da, soft ice cream"*) but superstar Adele loved it, commenting *"The chorus of this song makes me feel like I'm flying"*.

"[Salvatore is] probably the [one]
that's the most different from all the
other tracks on the record. [It has
an] Old World Italian feel." [172]

# - LANA DEL REY

Many have speculated that *24* was intended for the James Bond film, *Spectre*, but lost out to Sam Smith's *Writing's on the Wall*.

*Swan Song* re-sparked retirement rumours, not only due to the title but also the line *"and I will never sing again"*. Thankfully, this was quickly disproven.

"It's the antithesis of hopefulness. It's about trying to find beauty in giving up. If I had my way, I would continue to persist in all areas of my life, but it can be quite challenging because I can be too trusting too soon. The burn that can come from that really can incinerate your whole thinking life and your daily processes. At the end of every album, I say goodbye and thank you—very Old Hollywood style—and yet I cannot help but just continue to write." [173]

# - LANA DEL REY

Closing song *Don't Let Me Be Misunderstood* is a Nina Simone cover, much like *The Other Woman* ending *Ultraviolence*. It bears repeating that Lana has *Nina* tattooed on her chest.

## HONEYMOON UNRELEASED OUTTAKES

U p to six versions of the song *Beautiful People Beautiful Problems* exist, one being an outtake from *Honeymoon*. It was later recorded with Stevie Nicks for the *Lust for Life* album.

The *Ultraviolence* outtake Wild One was attempted again for *Honeymoon* then again for *Blue Banisters*, never arriving anywhere. The 2012 and 2015 versions leaked in 2021.

As previously noted, *Ultraviolence's Yes to Heaven* was also recorded for *Honeymoon* and *Lust for Life* but was scrapped the whole way. Some versions have leaked.

Other reported tracks include *If I Die Young, California* (not to be confused with the same-named song from *Norman Fucking Rockwell!*), *Crazy for You*, and *Dark City*.

# 8.2.
# TOUR: FESTIVAL TOUR

There was no official tour in support of *Honeymoon*, but Lana did embark on a tour around 14 festivals in 2016 through Europe and the Americas. Big names included *Rockwave Festival* in Malakasa, Greece, and *Lollapalooza* in Chicago, USA.

# 8.3.
# HI, HOW ARE YOU DANIEL JOHNSTON?

*H*i, *How Are You Daniel Johnston* is a 15-minute documentary film about... Daniel Johnston, a singer-songwriter famed for his childlike songs and psychiatric issues. Originally funded by a Kickstarter campaign, Lana Del Rey and rapper Mac Miller contributed $10,000 to the project, and both received producer credits. Lana felt particularly attached to the short, recording a cover of Johnston's *Some Things Last a Long Time* to be used in the film.

"It moved me. It was sad. It touched me. There were so many dimensions in one room: the past, the present at the time and then here he is right there *watching himself. I mean, I guess the one thing I hoped is that he understood that while he's home alone doing his art still—he says he writes every day— that he knows that he really did make a difference in people's lives. He made a difference in mine."* [174]

# - LANA DEL REY

The docco premiered on November 7, 2015, at Los Angeles' MAMA Gallery, where Lana got to meet Daniel Johnston for the first time. Due to her profound love for the man, Lana experienced the other side of the fan perspective.

*"I guess he was sort of a crush at one time a decade ago. It was so wonderful and sweet."* [175]

# - LANA DEL REY

Sadly, Johnston passed away two years later, making this time capsule moment all the more significant.

"Trying to choose the darkness or the light and sort of participating in the path that you're going to take, to the limited ability you can. I didn't know if this film would move me just as much, but the fact that it's a progression, it moves me even deeper." [176]

## - LANA DEL REY

Mac Miller also died a year later.

# 8.4.
# OVERDUE AWARDS FOR LANA

Lana's professional life continued to soar as she was rec-ognised by the Billboard Women in Music ceremony, winning the 2015 Trailblazer Award. Later, she also won the MTV Europe Music Award for Best Alternative Artist, her second time after 2012's success.

# 8.5.
# LANA ON THE WEEKND

The Weeknd has played a starring role in Lana's success, the lady herself admitting her big break largely came from his influence.

*"Me and my sister made a video for [Video Games] at home and then The Weeknd posted it on his Tumblr like 11 days in a row. I was like, 'oh my god'"* [177]

## - LANA DEL REY

On August 28, 2015, The Weeknd released his single *Prisoner* from the album *Beauty Behind the Madness*, which was co-written by and featured Lana. Critic reaction was positive, Bustle calling it *"dark, tortured, and a little bit over-the-top"*, while Rolling Stone described it as *"a summit of luxuriant sadness"* and *"quite the slow-burning pity party"*. Many fans have called it one of Lana's best collaborative pieces, which undoubtedly encouraged the two to pursue more creative projects together.

"Me and Lana have been friends for a long time. I've inspired her. She's inspired me. I feel like we've always been talking to each other through our music. She is the girl in my music, and I am the guy in her music. It's just this ghostly collaboration that feels the most natural on the whole [Beauty Behind the Madness] album. Even the whole monologue intro on Lonely Star from [my 2011 mixtape] Thursday. I just realised now that that's Lana. That's Lana's voice. I mean, it's my voice pitched up, but it's her. It's who she is. She was definitely *the first feature that I wanted to bring on this album."* [178]

## - THE WEEKND

Lana Del Rey and The Weeknd have since collaborated so many times that dual fans affectionately refer to her as Stargirl. This is due to her work on The Weeknd's 2016 album *Starboy*, where Lana provided lead vocals on *Stargirl Interlude* and co-wrote the record's third single *Party Monster*, which reached the Top 20 on the Billboard Hot 100, certified double-platinum in the USA. This would not be the last time the two worked together.

On a completely unrelated note, 2016 was also gifted with Smiler's mixtape *All I Know*, where the song *Big Spender* featured Lana's vocals. Strange to come out now, as the track was recorded way back in 2010.

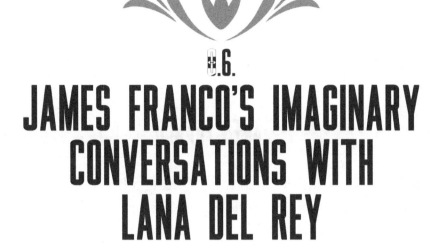

# #.6.
# JAMES FRANCO'S IMAGINARY CONVERSATIONS WITH LANA DEL REY

Lana and James Franco were long rumoured to be in a relationship due to the two hanging out in photos posted on their respective social medias. But according to Franco, it was never a romantic connection.

"We're friends [...] I'll tell you why,
maybe it's a boring answer. There's
a weird thing with creative types.
Sometimes I love a person's work and,
like, I'm just so enamoured with that
and their persona in their work. But
outside of that, it's like, our dynamic

is we're just kind of friends, we get along so well. But all this sexual attraction is for the person and the work. We go to Coney Island and hang out. I would have sex with her music." [179]

## - JAMES FRANCO

Still, this didn't stop Franco from writing a book about Lana titled *Flip-Side: Real and Imaginary Conversations with Lana Del Rey*. Set for a March 15, 2016 release, it was pushed back to May 9, 2017, and is now (most likely humorously) set on Amazon for a December 31, 2035 publication date. Most people, including Lana, doubt it will ever see even that deadline.

"I guess I was surprised there was a book. I haven't seen it. And I don't think it's gonna come out. It's a cool idea." [180]

## - LANA DEL REY

Lana went on to say:

"I thought it was cool that someone I really liked was writing a book about me, but then I had read an excerpt of it [...] I believe the title was like *Real and Imagined Conversations with Lana*, and we hadn't really spoken all that much. So I wasn't thrilled with the presentation, it was definitely a projection. So I said to him, 'maybe you should just write *Fake Conversations with Lana Del Rey*'." [181]

## - LANA DEL REY

# PART NINE
# LUST FOR LIFE ERA

# 9.1.
# ALBUM: LUST FOR LIFE (2017)

# LUST FOR LIFE (2017)

## 1. Love
*(co-written with Rick Nowels, Benjamin Levin, and Emile Haynie, first single)*

## 2. Lust for Life
*(featuring The Weeknd, co-written with Rick Nowels, Abel Tesfaye, and Max Martin, second single)*

## 3. 13 Beaches
*(co-written with Rick Nowels)*

## 4. Cherry
*(co-written with Tim Larcombe)*

## 5. White Mustang
*(co-written with Rick Nowels)*

## 6. Summer Bummer
*(featuring ASAP Rocky and Playboi Carti, co-written with Matthew Samuels, Rakim Mayers, Jordan Carter, Tyler Williams, Jahaan Sweet, Andrew Joseph Gradwohl Jr., third single)*

## 7. Groupie Love
*(featuring ASAP Rocky, co-written with Rick Nowels and Rakim Mayers, fourth single)*

## 8. In My Feelings
*(co-written with Rick Nowels)*

## 9. Coachella - Woodstock in My Mind
*(co-written with Rick Nowels)*

## 10. God Bless America - and All the Beautiful Women in It
*(co-written with Rick Nowels)*

## 11. When the World Was at War We Kept Dancing
*(co-written with Rick Nowels and Dean Reid)*

12. Beautiful People Beautiful Problems

*(featuring Stevie Nicks, co-written with Rick Nowels,*
*Justin Parker, and Stevie Nicks)*

13. Tomorrow Never Came

*(featuring Sean Ono Lennon, co-written with*
*Sean Ono Lennon and Rick Nowels)*

14. Heroin

*(co-written with Rick Nowels)*

15. Change

*(co-written with Rick Nowels)*

16. Get Free

*(co-written with Rick Nowels and Kieron Menzies)*

TOTAL RUNTIME: 72:08

*"I made my first 4 albums for me, but this one is for my fans and about where I hope we are all headed."* [182]

# - LANA DEL REY

Del Rey's fifth studio album, *Lust for Life*, was released on July 21, 2017, through Polydor and Interscope Records, while Urban Records dealt with some European distribution. It was recorded around Los Angeles (The Green Building, Record Plant), New York City (Electric Lady Studios, The Farm Studios), and London (Hampstead Studios, Sole Studios, Strongroom). Production was handled by the usual suspects (Rick Nowels, Kieron Menzies, and Emile Haynie) but also included newbies Boi-1da, Max Martin, Benny Blanco, and Metro Boomin.

*Lust For Life* was Lana's first record to feature guest artists, namely The Weeknd, A$AP Rocky, Stevie Nicks, Sean Lennon, and Playboi Carti.

The artwork was shot using Kodak Porta 800 film by Del Rey's sister, Chuck Grant. It was the first of her covers where she is seen smiling. Like *Honeymoon*, a promotional trailer was published to YouTube.

The sound drew parallels to *Born to Die*, in particular the poppy hip-hop beats. Genres identified include *"new-age folk"* (Billboard) and *"trap pop"* (Vulture).

"I started out thinking that the whole record was gonna have a sort of a '50s-'60s feeling, kind of Shangri-Las, early Joan Baez influences. But I don't know, as the climate kept on getting more heated politically, I found lyrically everything was just directed towards that. So because of that, the sound just got really updated, and I felt like it was more wanting to talk to the younger side of the audience *that I have. I guess it's a little more socially aware. It's kind of a global feeling."* [183]

# - LANA DEL REY

*Lust for Life* smashed the charts. It debuted at number one on the US Billboard 200 (107,000 units sold), her second album to do so. It was also her third number one on the UK Albums Chart. Other countries she topped included Australia, Canada, Croatia, Mexico, Norway, Portugal, Scotland, Spain, and Sweden. Furthermore, it reached the top three in Belgium, the Czech Republic, Finland, France, Ireland, New Zealand, Poland, and Switzerland.

Critic response was favourable albeit lesser enthusiastic than some of her earlier works. With an 83 score, Paste Magazine was concerned it felt *"bloated and sluggish at times and the hip-hop contributions by A$AP Rocky and Playboi Carti are ill-conceived"* but *"despite a handful of missteps, Del Rey continues to reinvent and redefine herself in new and captivating ways, and Lust For Life is just one more step in that profound and lovely evolution"*. Drowned In Sound gave it 80, stating, *"Lust for Life represents the thawing of the ice queen we thought we knew, and the strange death of her American dream. The warmth and humility revealed beneath are all the more thrilling for how well they were kept under lock and key. Human after all."* Many other publications scored the record 80, such as NME, Spin, The Observer, The Guardian, the Independent, The New York Times, and The Telegraph. On the flip side, No Ripcord

called it *"a scattered, confusing record"*, while American Songwriter said, *"the album is still painted in the same shades as Del
Rey's previous releases. At times it's some of her best material, but
it seems like a record best experienced in pieces than as a proper
whole"*, both awarding it 60. Metacritic's aggregate score landed on a 77, her second-highest to date and only one point below *Honeymoon*. Still, it's worth noting that with an 8.1 User
Score on that same platform, it is her worst according to the
general public.

    *Lust For Life* was nominated for the Grammy's 2018 Best
Pop Vocal Album but lost to Ed Sheeran's ÷. Many 2017 end-
of-year publications featured the album, most notably Noisey
(19), Cosmopolitan (9), Pitchfork (Pop and R&B Albums,
8), and Rolling Stone (Pop Albums, 2).

## LUST FOR LIFE SINGLES

*L*ove was the lead single, released on February 18, 2017, and
was instant hot stuff. Pitchfork felt it *"reassures the listener
that the feeling can still lift, that love can still conquer"*, awarding it the Best New Track status and listing it as the 28th-best
song of 2017. Rolling Stone called it *"anthemic"* and Vulture
called it *"marvellously good"*. Within 24 hours of release, it was
trending on Twitter. Debuting at number 44 on the Billboard
Hot 100 made it her highest since *West Coast*. It also reached
the top 10 in Belgium (9), Iceland (9), Hungary (4), Greece
(3), and New Zealand (3).

*"I'm glad it's the first thing out. It
doesn't sound that retro, but I was*

listening to a lot of Shangri-Las and wanted to go back to a bigger, more mid-tempo, single-y sound. The last 16 months, things were kind of crazy in the US, and in London when I was there. I was just feeling like I wanted a song that made me feel a little more positive when I sang it." [184]

# - LANA DEL REY

A music video was released on February 20, 2017, directed by Rich Lee. Here, a black and white Lana sings in front of a small audience while a full-coloured young couple floats through space. Later, Lana is performing on the moon, of course. Critics called it *"dreamy"* (Rolling Stone), *"romantic"* (Consequence), and a *"stunning sci-fi video"* (A.V Club).

The title track, *Lust for Life*, was the second single, released April 19, 2017. It was one of the first songs Del Rey wrote for the album but wasn't satisfied with its outcome. She brought it to producer Max Martin, who suggested she turn the verse into the chorus. She did so, and loved the new structure, deciding it would be perfect with contributions from The Weeknd, making it their fourth collaboration to date.

Critics were unsure about the song, most calling it a low point of the album. Paste said it *"did not work so well"*.

PopMatters considered it *"hollow"* compared with her former work. NME said Lana sounded like a *"parody of herself"*. Fortunately, not everyone agreed, Rolling Stone listing it as their 9th-best song of 2017. The song hit number 7 in Iceland as well as number 1 in Greece and New Zealand.

On May 22, 2017, another Clark Jackson-directed music video was released where Lana and The Weeknd cuddle and perform on the top of the *H* on the Hollywood sign. Much like the *Love* video, there are references to space dotted about. Viewers drew parallels between these visuals and British actress Peg Entwistle, who committed suicide by jumping from that very letter.

The first promotional single was *Coachella – Woodstock in My Mind*, released on May 15, 2017. In an Instagram post, Lana expressed her concerns with the festival scene's ignorant bliss within turbulent political climates.

"I'm not gonna lie, I had complex feelings about spending the weekend dancing whilst watching tensions [with] North Korea mount. It's a tightrope between being vigilantly observant of everything going on in the world and also having enough space and time to appreciate God's good earth the way it was intended to be appreciated. On my way home, I found myself compelled to visit an old favourite place of mine at the rim of the world highway where I took a moment to sit down by the sequoia grove and write a little song. I just wanted to share this in hopes that one individual's hope and prayer for peace might contribute to the possibility of it in the long run." [185]

## - LANA DEL REY

Critics approved, The Guardian calling it a *"sedated trap track"* while Exclaim! described it as *"an electronic spin on Lana's classic torch-song style"*.

"What a blessing it is to make music in general. And to have the freedom to put songs out about things that move me in real-time. I wrote one this last month on my way back from

*Coachella. Thank you to my producer and engineers for fixing it up so quickly. Hope you like it."* [186]

# - LANA DEL REY

*Summer Bummer* was the third single, released on July 12, 2017. Featuring A$AP Rocky and Playboi Carti, Pitchfork said their *"contributions feel a little unnecessary, as Del Rey has no trouble carrying a track on her own"*. Many other critics welcomed the hip-hop influences absent from her previous two records, and the song reached number two and three in New Zealand and Sweden, respectively. During the rushed preorder announcement, the song had a typo, listed as *Summer Bummber*. No known official video was produced.

Released on July 28, 2017, *Groupie Love* was the fourth single, another A$AP Rocky feature. This song was less well received, some stating that A$AP *"adds nothing"* (Consequence) while disliking his *"standard third verse rap feature, where any supposed romantic chemistry falls flat"* (Spin). Still, the Kiwis liked the song, and it hit number 8 in New Zealand.

In an interview on July, 2017, producer Rick Nowels told Genius that *Groupie Love* was one of the first songs they wrote for the album.

*"Lana had the idea to bring A$AP Rocky. He's a great guy, very smart*

*and creative. His producer Hector Delgado came in too and did the beats on the song and co-produced it with us."* [187]

# - RICK NOWELS

## OTHER NOTEWORTHY SONGS FROM LUST FOR LIFE

Del Rey expressed interest in creating a music video for *Cherry*, but no director liked her idea for it. Discussions took place with her sister to shoot one, but it was later scrapped with Lana announcing *"it's still not happening"*.

Despite not being a single, *White Mustang* received an official music video. Released on September 13, 2017, and directed by Rich Lee, viewers grew suspicious when Lana did not mouth any words from *White Mustang*'s lyrics in the clip. Her detective fans soon speculated that this video footage was recycled, intended for the outtake *The Next Best American Record* due to the visuals matching up much better with many of that song's lyrics. Furthermore, a behind-the-scenes video for the shoot revealed Lana singing part of *The Next Best American Record* too, fueling the theory. The latter song was eventually released as part of *Norman Fucking Rockwell!*.

Lana's past troubles with feminism seemed to come full circle with *God Bless America - and All the Beautiful Women in It.*

"I wrote God Bless America before the Women's Marches, but I could tell they were going to happen... I realised a lot of women were nervous about some of the bills that might get passed that would directly affect them. So yes, it's a direct response in anticipation of what I thought would happen, and what did happen." [188]

## - LANA DEL REY

Lana wanted to release the song as a single but her manager, Ben Mawson, did not think it was a good idea.

"It has some strong messaging. Some iconography, with Lady Liberty, fire escapes and the streets, and I do get a little New York feel when I listen back to it [...] Well, it's the 'God' word. But the phrase has wider meaning. It's more of a sentiment. When I wrote it, I didn't feel like it was confined to a

traditional portrait of the Lord, as
some sects might see it. It was more
like, 'fucking God bless us all and
let's hope we make it through this.'
When all the Women's Marches were
happening, I had already written this
song, because I had been hearing a lot
of things online. And I have a sister,
and a lot of girlfriends, who had a
lot of concerns about things that
were being said in the media by some
of our leaders. And I saw an instant
reaction from women, and I was like,
'Wow. There is no confusing how women
are feeling about the state of the
nation.' And so, without really trying
to, I felt compelled to just write a song
and say we are all concerned. And
it really made me think about my
relationship with women. And I felt
proud of myself, because I do love the

women in my life. And I take care
of them, and I ask them what they
think about music, and guys, and
problems, and I thought it was so cool
that I'm really right there in the same
boat with them." [189]

# - LANA DEL REY

Another social-political theme could be found on *When the World Was at War We Kept Dancing*.

"Well, I have a song that's quite aware
about the collective worry, about
whether this is the end of an era. It's
called When the World Was at War
We Kept Dancing. But I actually
went back and forth about keeping
it on the record, because I didn't
want it there if it would make
people feel worse instead of better.
It's not apathetic. The tone of the
production is very dark, and doesn't

lead to a fucking happy feeling. And
the question it poses. Is this the end of
America, of an era? Are we running
out of time with this person at the
helm of a ship? Will it crash? In my
mind, the lyrics were a reminder not
to shut down or shut off, or just don't
talk about things. It was more, like,
stay vigilant and keep dancing.
Stay awake." [190]

# - LANA DEL REY

*Beautiful People Beautiful Problems* will go down in history as
the Lana Del Rey/Stevie Nicks song, featuring the Fleetwood
Mac legend herself.

"I didn't know what to expect or that
I could even ask her. When I went
through ideas of women that could
really add something to the record, she
was the one we kept coming back to.
'Bonafide badass' is a great phrase

for her. She was amazing, she's just everything you hope she's gonna be. She loved the track, and she added so much to it." [190] [191]

## - LANA DEL REY

Meanwhile, *Tomorrow Never Came* was also big talk in the guest star department, featuring the son of John Lennon and Yoko Ono, Sean Ono Lennon. Interestingly, the song included the lyric, *"I wish we could go back to your country house and put on the radio and listen to our favourite song by Lennon and Yoko"*.

"I didn't want him to think I was asking him because I was name-checking them. Actually, I had listened to his records over the years and I did think it was his vibe, so I played it for him and he liked it." [192]

## - LANA DEL REY

"I thought it might be strange for Sean to sing a song about John and

Yoko as well. But I think the fact that I sing, 'Isn't life crazy now that I'm singing with Sean.' It points to the fact that we're both aware. I didn't want it to come out exploitative in any fashion. Not that it would. Still, I wanted to be as careful as possible. I wanted it to come across layered with this sort of meta-narrative mixed in. In a way, it's a song about a song." [193]

# - LANA DEL REY

Sean was honoured by the request, saying the experience helped him to feel more satisfied with his vocal abilities.

*Heroin* was written about Rob Dubuss, one of Lana's exes, who died from a heroin overdose in 2011. Lana later revealed that her old song *Yayo* was about him too.

According to Rick Nowels, they started recording *Change* at 8:00 p.m. and by 2:00 a.m, it was finished, and the completed album was sent to the record label that same day. Pop-Crush called the song *"her most powerful and heartbreaking as she attempts to be honest, capable, and beautiful in the face of instability"*. Pitchfork agreed, saying it was the *"most stunning and thematically essential"* song on the record. It was used in a commercial for Youi, an Australian insurance company.

"[It's] feeling like you have to change on many different levels. First of all, that something has to change in the world. In the first verse, I sing, 'there's something in the wind, I can feel it blowing in', and in the second verse I sing that it's 'on the wings of a song'. When I express my thoughts about change through lyrics and music, it can be about North Korea launching missiles or whatever, but it can also be directed inwards. So in the second verse, I make it personal, when it's about being stable, strong, and secure, and not looking for new discoveries when I don't even have my shit together." [194]

## – LANA DEL REY

The final word on the album's final song, *Get Free*, is *"blue"* which Lana felt was a good omen as *"a little jumping off point for the next record"*.

"When I was writing that song, I had a little conversation with my engineer, who's one of my dear friends; his name's Kieron Menzies. And we were talking about this model they use in literature; sometimes it's called the Hero's Journey. And it starts with crossing the threshold of the ordinary world and moving to the main character's reveal of the heart. And then the character goes through all these different cycles; they battle the giant, they battle themselves, and then they come back and they find out who they really are. And so I liked that idea. I thought it sort of resembled my story. I revealed *my heart. And then the rest is a mystery."* [195]

## - LANA DEL REY

Two words are censored on the track, which were later revealed to be "Amy" and "Whitney", female icons who have their names tattooed on Lana's chest.

*"It's about people who don't get to reach their full potential because they let controlling people stop them from being free. [The Key is] going deeper. Knowing that you're your own doorway to the answers and not looking for answers in other people... taking the time to get to know yourself."* [196]

## - LANA DEL REY

The Fader magazine called it the best song on *Lust for Life*. Unfortunately, not everyone was impressed, which we shall address in the next chapter.

## LUST FOR LIFE UNRELEASED OUTTAKES

Lana appeared very excited for a song named *Roses Bloom for You* (which some suggest was meant to be the opening song on *Lust for Life*), but it was ultimately excluded. Only snippets have been released to the public.

"So many songs left on the cutting room floor but this was a special one I wrote in March called Roses Bloom For You. I don't film all my live takes but I'm glad I got this one because I was very excited about the beautiful chords my producer Rick Nowels found for this gem." [197]

## - LANA DEL REY

*Lust for Life* makes the final desperate attempt at getting a satisfactory version of *Yes to Heaven* on an album, but for the third time in a row, the record said no.

*Valley of the Dolls* was scrapped. The song was also rumoured to be considered for the later *Norman Fucking Rockwell!* album. It leaked in 2021.

*LA Who Am I* was considered for inclusion. Fans suggest this ultimately became her poem *LA Who Am I to Love You* found in the later book/spoke word record *Violet Bent Back-*

*wards Over the Grass.*

Two cut songs named *The Next Best American Record* and *Yosemite* were described by Lana as *"brother and sister"* tracks but felt their moods did not fit the overall record. They were both used on later albums (*Norman Fucking Rockwell!* and *Chemtrails Over the Country Club* respectively).

Other gone songs include *Serene Queen* and *Sugary Sweet*.

# 9.2.
# RADIOHEAD LAWSUIT

In January 2018, Del Rey revealed that a lawsuit between her and Radiohead alleged she had stolen her *Get Free* verse melodies from their hit song *Creep*. She claimed the band rejected her offer of 40% royalties as they wanted *"100%"*.

*"I just want to let you know that regardless of what happens in court, the sentiment that I wrote in that particular song, which was my statement song for the record, my personal manifesto, my modern manifesto. I just want to let you know*

*that regardless if it gets taken down off of everything, those sentiments that I wrote, I really am still gonna strive for them even if that song is not on the future physical releases of the record."* [198]

# - LANA DEL REY

Radiohead publisher Warner/Chappell denied the accusations.

*"It's true that we've been in discussions since August of last year with Lana Del Rey's representatives. It's clear that the verses of Get Free use musical elements found in the verses of Creep and we've requested that this be acknowledged in favour of all writers of Creep [...] To set the record straight, no lawsuit has been issued and Radiohead have not said they*

'will only accept 100 percent' of the publishing of Get Free." [199]

## - WARNER/CHAPPELL MUSIC

During her slot at Lollapalooza festival in São Paulo, Brazil, Lana casually announced that the conflict was over. The agreed terms are unknown as Radiohead remain uncredited on the track.

"Well, fuck, now that my lawsuit's over, I guess I can sing that song any time I want, right?" [200]

## - LANA DEL REY

# 9.3.
# TOUR: LA TO THE MOON TOUR

Following on from *Lust for Life*'s subtle space themes, Lana went on her fourth headlining concert tour named *LA to the Moon* which did not actually go to the moon, instead taking her across North America, South America, Oceania, and Europe. Support acts included Jhené Aiko, Kali Uchis, and Børns. It ran through 38 shows from January 5th to August 10th, earning $22.5 million along the way. Her final planned Israel show was cancelled due to the Israeli–Palestinian conflict.

# 9.4.
# SHELVED LAST SHADOW PUP-PETS COLLABORATIVE ALBUM

The Last Shadow Puppets are a supergroup featuring Alex Turner (Arctic Monkeys), Miles Kane (The Rascals, solo artist), James Ford (Simian, Simian Mobile Disc), and Zach Dawes (Mini Mansions). Around 2017, the band and Lana jammed together, recording an unknown amount of songs.

*"We had a little rock band on the side. It kind of didn't go anywhere but we had a good time. We were very messy!"* [201]

## - LANA DEL REY

One song they wrote, *California*, was later reworked for *Norman Fucking Rockwell!*. A rumoured unchanged song called *Dealer* made it onto *Blue Banisters* (complete with uncredited Miles Kane vocals). Similarly, the *Blue Banisters'* song *Thunder* was possibly written during these sessions. The ever-elusive *Yes to Heaven* may have been attempted by the band.

Another gossiped song, *Loaded*, was eventually released by Miles Kane for his 2018 album *Coup de Grace*, featuring vocals from Lana. An assumed track named *Dope* remains un-leaked.

## 9.5.
# 2018 GUEST VOCALS

If you were seeking a Lana fix in 2018, you'd have to find her on the work of others. These slots include:

- *Living with Myself* by Jonathan Wilson (*Rare Birds*, 2018)
- *God Save Our Young Blood* by Børns (*Blue Madonna*, 2018)
- *Blue Madonna* by Børns (*Blue Madonna*, 2018)
- *Woman* by Cat Power (*Wanderer*, 2018)

She also covered Andrew Lloyd Webber's *You Must Love Me*, originally performed by Madonna as part of the *Evita* soundtrack. Lana's version was released for Lloyd Webber's greatest hits album *Unmasked: The Platinum Collection*.

"Andrew Lloyd Webber has been one of my primary inspirations in music, so to do a cover of one of his songs is a dream. I especially love You Must Love Me, because of how unique the melody is. I've been incredibly inspired by all of Andrew's work from Phantom of the Opera to Evita." [202]

## - LANA DEL REY

# 9.6.
# 2019 ODD JOBS

As Lana's sixth studio album loomed over the horizon, she found time to present filmmaker Guillermo del Toro with his Hollywood Walk of Fame star on August 6, 2019. She further honoured del Toro with a Donovan cover of *Season of the Witch* for his film *Scary Stories to Tell in the Dark*.

Shortly following, Lana released the standalone single *Looking for America* as a response to the mass shootings in El Paso and Dayton. Critics praised the track, calling it *"poignant"* (Los Angeles Times) and *"timeless"* (MTV). MuuMuse stated it was *"beyond just being a beautiful, classically wistful, hauntingly sung Lana song about less worrisome days gone by while longing for a more peaceful future."*

# PART TEN
# NORMAN FUCKING ROCKWELL! ERA

# 10.1.
# ALBUM: NORMAN FUCKING ROCKWELL! (2019)

# NORMAN FUCKING ROCKWELL! (2019)

### 1. Norman fucking Rockwell
*(co-written with Jack Antonoff)*

### 2. Mariners apartment complex
*(co-written with Jack Antonoff, first single)*

### 3. Venice bitch
*(co-written with Jack Antonoff, second single)*

### 4. Fuck it I love you
*(co-written with Jack Antonoff, Andrew Watt, and Louis Bell, fifth single)*

### 5. Doin' Time
*(Sublime cover, written by Bradley Nowell, Rick Rubin, Adam Horovitz, Adam Yauch, Marshall Goodman, Ira Gershwin, DuBose Heyward, Dorothy Heyward, George Gershwin, fourth single, previously released for the Sublime documentary)*

### 6. Love song
*(co-written with Jack Antonoff)*

### 7. Cinnamon Girl
*(co-written with Jack Antonoff)*

### 8. How to disappear
*(co-written with Jack Antonoff)*

### 9. California
*(co-written with Zachary Dawes)*

### 10. The Next Best American Record
*(co-written with Rick Nowels)*

### 11. The greatest
*(co-written with Jack Antonoff, sixth single)*

### 12. Bartender
*(co-written with Rick Nowels)*

### 13. Happiness is a butterfly
*(co-written with Jack Antonoff and Rick Nowels)*

## 14. hope is a dangerous thing for a woman like me to have – but I have it

*(co-written with Jack Antonoff, third single)*

## TOTAL RUNTIME: 67:43

*"I wasn't feeling any pressure to make this album bigger or better than any of the rest of them. I was just having fun in the studio with Jack Antonoff. I was actually pretty thrilled at some of the melodies that were coming through as I was writing and just the sexy and cool all-natural vibe that was shaping up within the record as I was finishing it. You always hope a low-key record feels organic and for me this one really does."* [203]

# - LANA DEL REY

On August 30, 2019, Lana Del Rey's sixth studio album, *Norman Fucking Rockwell!*, arrived. It was released through Polydor and Interscope Records and produced by Jack Antonoff. Other production credits go to Zach Dawes,

Andrew Watt, and our pal Rick Nowels. Recordings took place in many studios around Los Angeles (Conway, Westlake, Henson, Gold Tooth, Valentine, Sunset Banana Split), Seattle (House of Breaking Glass), New York City (Electric Lady, Rough Customer) and London (SARM, Hampstead).

The title is a reference to painter and illustrator Norman Rockwell.

> "It was kind of an exclamation mark: so this is the American dream, right now. This is where we're at. Norman fucking Rockwell. We're going to go to Mars, and Trump is president, all right." [204]

## - LANA DEL REY

The comic-styled cover art was taken by her sister, Chuck Grant, and features Lana standing on a boat with Duke Nicholson (grandson of Jack Nicholson). A promotional trailer for the album was released on August 1, 2019.

*Norman Fucking Rockwell!* marks a shift in Lana's sound, most likely owed to new producer Jack Antonoff's influence, who plays drums, piano, guitar, and synths on the record. The result has been called soft rock and psych-rock, with plenty of piano ballads.

The record debuted at number 3 on the US Billboard 200 chart (104,000 sales), marking Del Rey's sixth US top ten. Elsewhere, it shot up the charts, hitting number 1 in Argentina, Estonia, Lithuania, Portugal, Scotland, Switzerland, UK, and US Billboard Alternative Albums. Additionally, it reached the top 5 in Australia, Belgium, Canada, the Czech Republic, Denmark, The Netherlands, France, Germany, Greece, Ireland, Italy, Mexico, New Zealand, Norway, Poland, Spain, and Sweden.

Critical response to *Norman Fucking Rockwell!* can only be described as an avalanche of worship to the likes no album from her career has received. Both NOW and NME awarded it full marks, whereas notoriously hard-to-please Pitchfork gave it a 94 (*"Lana Del Rey sings exquisitely of freedom and transformation and the wreckage of being alive. It establishes her as one of America's greatest living songwriters."*) which came with its revered Best New Music badge of honour. With a 90 score, Rolling Stone claimed Del Rey *"has finally made her pop classic"*. Other 90+s include AllMusic, DIY Magazine, Variety, PopMatters, Glide Magazine, No Ripcord, and Consequence.

Naturally, you can't please all of the people all of the time, and The Guardian disregarded the record as a *"beguiling and frustrating experience"* while The Telegraph called Lana at risk of being *"just another over sensitive and particularly self-absorbed singer-songwriter"*. No matter, as Metacritic aggregated the overall score as 87, Lana's highest to date.

Also according to Metacritic, *Norman Fucking Rockwell!* was featured in more year-end rankings than any other 2019 album. Despite Guardian's earlier gripes, they later called it the Best Album of 2019. Other similar placements include Pitchfork (1), Slant (1), NME (3), Rolling Stone (3), Time (4), Juice Nothing (4), Billboard (6), and Entertainment Weekly (9). Even more significant, it made many end-of-decade lists, such as Pitchfork (19), Uproxx (15), and Slant Magazine (3). Rolling Stone went one step further and named it the 321st Greatest Album of All Time. The album was nominated for the 2020 Album of the Year Grammy but lost to Billie Eilish's debut *When We All Fall Asleep, Where Do We Go?*. It did, however, win NME's Best Album of 2020.

## NORMAN FUCKING ROCKWELL! SINGLES

*M*ariners Apartment Complex led the single way, released on September 12, 2018. Much like all things *Norman Fucking Rockwell!*, the song was showered with unanimous acclaim. Billboard noted the *"wondrous whispers and dreamy layered harmonies about a beautiful, yet tumultuous, romance"*. Rolling Stone compliments *"Negating her earliest works, growing out of her previous attitudes and forsaking the image of the Good American Girl looking for a figure to make her feel wanted, desired and cool"*. Spin said she *"offers everything: her power as a cypher and her vulnerability as an individual, bottled up tight in the character of Lana Del Rey and cast into the waves"*. It was rated the 29th best song of 2018 by Consequence and 6th by Rolling Stone.

"The song is about this time I took a walk late at night with a guy I was seeing, and we stopped in front his friend's apartment complex, and he put his hand around my shoulder, and he said 'I think we are together because we're both similar, like we're both really messed up' and I thought it was the saddest thing I'd ever heard. And I said, 'I'm not sad, I didn't know that's why you thought you were relating to me on that level, I'm actually doing pretty good'. And he was upset, and that's when I wrote the song. I thought I had to sort of step on that role where I was showing the way and I was sort of being the brighter light." [205]

# - LANA DEL REY

The simplistic music video was filmed by Lana's sister, Chuck Grant, and features two females playing with butterflies as stock clips of the ocean crashes into the rocks.

*Venice Bitch* was the second single, released less than a week later, on September 18, 2018. At nine minutes and thirty-six seconds long, it was Del Rey's longest track at that point.

*"I played it for my managers and I was like, 'yeah I think this is the single I want to put out. And they were like, 'It's 10 minutes long, are you kidding me? It's called Venice Bitch. Like why do you do this to us? Can you make a three-minute normal pop song?' I was like, 'well, end of summer, some people just wanna drive around for 10 minutes and get lost in some electric guitar'."* [206]

## - LANA DEL REY

The song instantly wiped the floor with the critics. Pitchfork said Lana *"has never allowed herself to sink so completely into an atmosphere, burrowing deep into the song's dark blue, moody grooves"* and awarded it the Best New Track honour. Rolling Stone reckoned it *"might be the most expansive California beach record ever made, and not just for its length"*, adding in a separate review, *"it's the most experimental music she's ever made, and finally fades out after nine and a half minutes. And still it feels too short"*. Noisey said it *"feels like an encapsulation of all of the romance we associate with her, and has a distinct sense of the passage of time, capturing her where she is now"*. It hit various Best Songs of 2018 lists, for example, Idolator (1), Crack Magazine

(2), Spin (3), and Noisey (4).

"Venice Bitch. I have quite a grounded but surreal impression of LA day to day. I love the friendships and organic relationships I have here, but I also love how dramatic the landscape of the city is on the outer edges." [207]

# - LANA DEL REY

Like *Mariners*, the music video was directed by Chuck Grant, where vintage-style footage speeds a freeway by as Lana hangs around like a home video.

*Hope Is a Dangerous Thing for a Woman Like Me to Have – but I Have It* worked as the third single, released on January 9, 2019. It was originally titled (and inspired by) *Sylvia Plath*. Lana's high roll continued, as critics were swept up by the *"exceptionally crafted"* song (Spin), everyone agreeing on its *"mournful"* meditations (Rolling Stone) where Lana was *"delivering one of her most confessional offerings to date"* (NME). Billboard called it Lana's best song ever, describing it as the *"most vulnerable moment in Lana Del Rey's discography, and the most truthful"*.

"It was staggered with references from living in Hollywood and seeing so many things that didn't look right to me, things that I never thought I'd have permission to talk about, because everyone knew and no one ever said anything. The culture only changed in the last two years as to whether people would believe you. And I've been in this business now for 15 years! So I was writing a song to myself. Hope truly is a dangerous thing for a woman like me to have, because I know so much. But I have it." [208]

# - LANA DEL REY

A homemade video was released on August 25, 2021.

Way back when, on May 17, 2019, Lana released a cover of Sublime's *Doin' Time* for the *Sublime* documentary, which later functioned as *Norman Fucking Rockwell!*'s fourth single (August 29, 2019). Everyone loved it, from the former members of Sublime to every critic under the sky, receiving praiseworthy descriptions such as *"glittering"* (Rolling Stone) and *"very, very good"* (Stereogum). The Fader even went as far as to say Lana's version *"improves upon the original"*. Sublime drummer Bud Gaugh said the *"smoky, sexy, and iconic sound of her voice breathes new life into one of our favourite singles"*, and the widow of Sublime frontman Bradley Nowell, Troy Dendekker, said it was *"an honour to have [Del Rey's] talent complement the Sublime legacy"*.

"I did that song because the label I'm signed to is producing the documentary about Sublime's life story. So they asked a bunch of people to cover different songs, and I obviously said yes and went down. But I definitely thought about it just because I do love Sublime so much. It was probably one of the few things I don't want to fuck up [...] I listen to a Sublime track probably every day driving, [it] makes me feel cool, and even when it's in my tracklisting I'm like, 'oh god, it's the coolest one.'" [209]

## - LANA DEL REY

The music video resembled the *Attack of the 50-Foot Woman* film, where a giant Lana walks across recognisable Los Angeles locations, causing trouble. This turns out to be a movie within the video, where a different version of Lana is watching the flick at the drive-in. No spoilers, but these two worlds eventually interact in a hilarious manner.

Before any of these official singles blessed our ears, *Fuck It I Love You* and *The Greatest* were released together as promotional tracks on August 22, 2019. Both songs were adored. *The Greatest*, in particular, appeared to capture the biggest net of imagination, NME calling it *"maybe one of the greatest songs she's ever written"* while it received the Pitchfork stamp of Best New Track approval, dubbing it the 79th Best Song of the 2010s. As for *Fuck It I Love You*, Chad Smith of the Red Hot Chili Peppers plays drums on it.

In an interview with The Washington Post, Del Rey commented on *The Greatest* lyric *"Dennis' last stop before Kokomo"*:

*"I literally went on a date [in Marina del Rey], and this dude was trying to impress me and was like, 'This was Dennis' last stop before he hit his head on the dock'."* [210]

## - LANA DEL REY

These two tracks were released as a 9-minute double-feature

music video directed by Rich Lee. In what's considered by some a short film, Lana fake-surfs with model Brad Swanick in a 1960's type aesthetic then sings in front of a neon backdrop and wanders the Long Beach harbour.

## OTHER NOTEWORTHY SONGS FROM NORMAN FUCKING ROCKWELL!

*"Goddamn man-child. You fucked me so good that I almost said, 'I love you'."*

# - LANA DEL REY

(LYRICS FROM *NORMAN FUCKING ROCKWELL*)

The title and opening track, *Norman Fucking Rockwell*, was another much-praised song on the album, even nominated for Song of the Year at the 62nd Annual Grammy Awards but losing again to Billie Eilish (with *Bad Guy*). It hit number 8 on New Zealand Hot Singles charts.

The song also features the lyric *"As you colour me blue"*, which appears to lead directly on from the end of her previous album, *Lust for Life*, where the very last word is blue too (*"a little jumping off point for the next record"*).

*"Working with Jack Antonoff, I was in a little bit of a lighter mood because he was so funny. So the title*

*track is called 'Norman Fucking Rockwell', and it's kind of about this guy who is such a genius artist, but he thinks he's the shit. He knows it and he, like, won't shut up talking about it."* [211]

## - LANA DEL REY

On December 21, 2019, a 14-minute 3-part home video appeared, directed by Chuck Grant and featuring *Norman Fucking Rockwell, Bartender,* and *Happiness Is a Butterfly.*

During an Instagram livestream, Lana mentioned the possibility of a *Love Song* video, but it has yet to manifest.

*"I feel like Love Song is the kind of song you have to have a video for, to realise that it's kinda special—'cause otherwise it's pretty stark. I'd like to paint it, like have a painted video, like a Monet that came to life."* [212]

## - LANA DEL REY

*Cinnamon Girl* was considered a standout track by several

critics, loved as a slightly different style from the rest of the record. That is, except for NPR critic Ann Powers who enjoyed the album but gave this particular song a harsh review, stating (among other things) that the track:

"...is slippery, unattached to the process of telling a story [and it] feels more like you're in a story, in someone's head at a particularly unsure moment. A great songwriter, as we tend to understand that role, would offer a more coherent view. But for Del Rey, the mash-up of effects and references is the point. It is emotion's actuality." [213]

# - ANN POWERS
(NPR REVIEW)

Lana lashed back on Twitter with:

"I don't even relate to one observation you made about the music. There's nothing uncooked about me. To write *about me is nothing like it is to be with me. Never had a persona. Never needed one. Never will [...] So don't call yourself a fan like you did in the article and don't count your editor one either. I may never never have made bold political or cultural statements before, because my gift is the warmth I live my life with and the self reflection I share generously."* [214]

# - LANA DEL REY

Bloodthirsty fans quickly came to Lana's side and bullied Powers until she decided to take some time off social media. This caused a ricochet backlash for Lana, whereby people felt she should have been more open to criticism. During this conflict, both *Ann Powers* and *Cinnamon Girl* rose as trending topics on Twitter.

*California* shares its name with another unreleased track from the *Honeymoon* sessions, but they are different songs. Reportedly, a homemade video was filmed but never came to light. It was confirmed to be written as part of the unreleased The Last Shadow Puppets sessions.

As previously stated, *The Next Best American Record* was originally intended for *Lust For Life* but was deemed unsuitable for that record's mood, finding itself here instead. The video for *White Mustang* is long rumoured to be shot for this song but repurposed for the former.

*Bartender* claims a segment of the 3-part music video with *Norman Fucking Rockwell* and *Happiness Is a Butterfly*. Scenes from this piece were first introduced in the *Venice Bitch* video.

## NORMAN FUCKING ROCKWELL! UNRELEASED OUTTAKES

*Not All Who Wander Are Lost* was originally recorded for *Norman Fucking Rockwell!*, but was instead released unchanged on *Chemtrails Over the Country Club*.

*Lust for Life*'s scrapped *Valley of the Dolls* was rumoured to be considered the *Norman Fucking Rockwell!* album too. It leaked in 2021.

*Hey Blue Baby* and *I Must Be Stupid for Being so Happy* were recorded together with Jack Antonoff for the 5th Ally Coalition Show (hosted by Antonoff). While the sessions appear to crossover with *Norman Fucking Rockwell!*, Lana has stated that they were written exclusively for the show.

# 10.2.
# MEET JACK ANTONOFF

"I had met him [in the] elevator at Emil Haney's Studio who helped produce one of my first albums. [And then] I met Jack again a year and a half ago, and he's, like, 'Remember me and the guys from Fun? We all had our glasses on, and we were like... hi, Lana!' As he said that, I vividly remember three sweet guys with the *glasses being like, 'Hi, we love Video Games!'* [215]

## - LANA DEL REY

Jack Michael Antonoff is the lead singer of Bleachers and the guitarist/drummer in the band Fun. However, he is far better known for his eight-time Grammy Award-winning production work. Before collaborating with Lana Del Rey, he had already created magic for Carly Rae Jepsen, Sia, and Lorde (in particular, her 2017 masterpiece, *Melodrama*). But it's his multiple songs with Taylor Swift that have risen Jack as one of the most desirable producers on the scene, with his name smeared across *1989*, *Reputation*, *Lover*, *Folklore*, and *Midnights* (to name only some). For these exact credentials, Lana was unsure about their creative partnership.

*"He wanted me to meet him in some random diner, and I was like, 'You already worked with everyone else, I don't know where there's room for me'."* [216]

## - LANA DEL REY

Thankfully, Antonoff managed to win her over by playing her some atmospheric riffs that helped clear a mental path for the *Norman* project.

"For the first few months I worked with [Antonoff], he would play me, like, five chords in a row that would end up becoming a new song each time, and I would ask him, like, 'are you sure I'm allowed to have this? Do you not wanna save that progression for yourself?' and he thought that was hilarious; he was like, 'No, I've been dying to meet you and give you this'." [217]

## - LANA DEL REY

On July 30, 2021, Jack Antonoff's band, Bleachers, released their third album called *Take the Sadness Out of Saturday Night*. This business is about who you know; hence the relatively overlooked album managed to pull some hefty strings, and Lana was featured on the promotional single *Secret Life*.

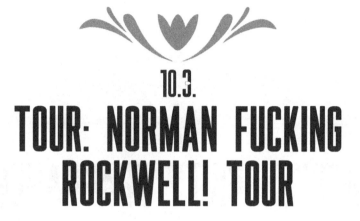

# 10.3.
# TOUR: NORMAN FUCKING ROCKWELL! TOUR

Lana's fifth headlining concert tour ran from September 21 to November 30, 2019. It consisted of 18 shows in the US, one in Vancouver, Canada, and one in Abu Dhabi, UAE. Guest appearances included Sean Ono Lennon, Weyes Blood, Julia Jacklin, Nikki Lane, and Chris Isaak. An additional 21 shows were cancelled either from Lana falling ill or the COVID pandemic. Regardless, the tour grossed $2,479,294.

# 10.4.
# GUCCI'S GUILTY FRAGRANCES

In November 2019, Lana Del Rey and Jared Leto were announced as the faces of Gucci's Guilty Fragrances.

*"[Gucci] wanted to have a campaign that was centred around this concept of 'Hollyweird' so I guess [they] thought I was just weird enough for it."* [218]

## - LANA DEL REY

Through print and TV ads, Lana and Jared go about their daily chores, such as folding laundry and grocery shopping. Lana's pal, Courtney Love, makes a cameo as a waitress, while an ostrich is seen in the store.

*"Yes, having Courtney anywhere is totally fabulous. I love that girl and I am always happy when I see her. She is somebody I chat with on the phone and love catching up with her. But she's definitely a Hollywood icon, and a music icon, so I was thrilled she was gonna be a part of it."* [218]

# - LANA DEL REY

Creative director Alessandro Michele stated that Guilty is a scent for a woman who does whatever she wants. Lana Del Rey agreed that she is *"very much that person"*.

# 10.5.
# CHARLIE'S ANGELS

A lead single for the 2019 *Charlie's Angels* reboot was required. They named it *Don't Call Me Angel* and featured the powerhouse trio of Ariana Grande, Miley Cyrus, and... Lana Del Rey, obviously. Released on September 13, 2019, the song hit the top 10 in Australia (4), Canada (7), Czech Republic (3), Estonia (4), Finland (9), Greece (1), Hungary (1), Iceland (1), Ireland (2), Israel (1), Lebanon (1), Lithuania (3), Malaysia (7), New Zealand (6), Portugal (8), Scotland (1), Serbia (3), Singapore (3), Slovakia (3), Switzerland (4), and the UK (2). But the critical world did not reflect the commercial success, as many reviewers were unsure about the stylistic differences between the artists, lacking a certain natural chemistry.

A music video was released on the same day, where the three artists dance around wearing wings while Miley beats up a guy on a chair and Lana throws a knife into the groin area of a dummy target practice.

"The song's really cute. When I first heard it, obviously I wasn't on it, it was just Ariana's part and they wanted me to write something. So I cut her verse into a half-time bridge and just [said] some stuff over her choruses as well. And then Miley jumped on. It's just really very spicy." [219]

## - LANA DEL REY

# 10.6.
# RANDOM PROJECTS

On November 28, 2019, Amazon Prime subscribers were treated to *The Kacey Musgraves Christmas Show* which came with a soundtrack of the same name. Like most Christmas cash-grabs, it received lukewarm reviews, but at least Lana featured, covering *I'll Be Home for Christmas* with Kacey, a song first made famous by Bing Crosby.

Around this time, Lana announced that she was working on a Broadway musical which she *"may finish in two or three years"* as well as contributing to the soundtrack of a new adaptation of *Alice's Adventures in Wonderland.* Both have yet to materialise.

*"It's more about the story of the author and the real-life Alice back*

in Cambridge. I have to learn a lot
more about it, but the songs are
really sweet." [220]

# - LANA DEL REY

On September 24, 2020, a remix of Matt Maeson's song *Hallucinogenics* dropped, featuring a newly added Lana voice. Critics widely praised how well their vocals worked together.

## 10.7.
# BOOK/ALBUM: VIOLET BENT BACKWARDS OVER THE GRASS (2020)

# VIOLET BENT BACKWARDS OVER THE GRASS (2020)

1. LA Who Am I to Love You
2. The Land of 1,000 fires
3. Violet bent backwards over the grass
4. Past the bushes cypress thriving
5. Salamander
6. Never to Heaven
7. Sportcruiser
8. Tessa Dipietro
9. Quiet Waiter Blue Forever
10. What happened when I left you
11. Happy
12. My Bedroom is a Sacred Place Now - There Are Children at the Foot of my Bed
13. Paradise is Very Fragile
14. Bare feet on linoleum

### TOTAL RUNTIME: 38:50

On July 9, 2020, Lana published her first book, *Violet Bent Backwards Over the Grass*. Featuring 30 of her poems and photography, it was accompanied by a spoken word album of 14 poems, which was backed by the music of Jack Antonoff, released on July 28, 2020. It was published by Simon & Schuster, and half of the proceeds went to the Navajo Water Project. The cover artwork is an orange tree painted by Erika Lee Sears.

This undertaking was born out of writer's block during the *Norman Fucking Rockwell!* age. Lana originally announced that she would bind the book herself and sell them for as little as a dollar each because *"my thoughts are priceless"*. This changed when Simon & Schuster acquired the rights and wanted to make money, charging full price.

"Someone asked me what my favourite album was that I'd made and my first thought was my poetry album, actually [...] if you like an artist, someone's innermost thoughts, and the way they speak through their thought process, [poetry] is a way to get to know them." [221]

# - LANA DEL REY

The Line of Best Fit said the album gave *"us a much clearer understanding of her than her songs are able to"*, while The Quietus called it *"one of the most fully formed albums she has put out"*, even if the reviewer found the rhymes *"clunky and a tad juvenile"*. Both awarded it 80. Meanwhile, DIY Magazine was more critical, stating it was a *"sixth former trying their best to impress at their first slam poetry event"* with 60. Metacritic aggregator scored it a 72 overall. At the time of writing this biography, *Violet Bent Backwards Over the Grass* holds a 3.93 score out of 5 on Goodreads. The album hit number 7 in Portugal, and the vinyl reached number 3 on the Billboard US Vinyl Albums chart.

## FACE MASK CONTROVERSY

On October 3, 2020, Lana held a surprise *Violet Bent Backwards Over the Grass* reading at a Barnes & Nobles in Los Angeles. This event was eventually shut down for not following COVID health regulations, which some claimed was due to Lana's mesh mask as it clearly exposed her nose and mouth. Lana responded that her mask had *"plastic on the inside"*.

"They're commonly sewn in by stylists these days. I don't generally respond to articles because I don't care. But there ya go. Same goes for everyone's masks in my video. I'm lucky enough to have a team of people who can do that." [222]

# - LANA DEL REY

# 10.⚓.
# SUPPORT LIVERPOOL AND YOU'LL NEVER WALK ALONE

Lana proudly supports Liverpool Football Club. She visited their home stadium at Anfield in 2013, where she was interviewed for their website.

*"Liverpool are my team but I also support Celtic in Scotland, who are my boyfriend Barrie [James O'Neill] 's team."* [223]

## - LANA DEL REY

On December 4, 2020, Lana released a cover of *You'll Never Walk Alone*. Originally from the 1945 Rodgers and Hammerstein musical *Carousel*, it has become a football anthem developed at Liverpool F.C., now their motto. Lana's version was used in the soundtrack for the club's documentary *The End Of The Storm*. All profits made went to the LFC foundation.

# 10.9.
# AMERICAN STANDARDS
# AND CLASSICS

At the end of 2020, Lana announced a Christmas day release of a digital album featuring *"American standards and classics"*, most likely called *Pacific Blue*.

"Somewhere in the back of my mind,
Ive been coordinating this concept
covers album called Pacific Blue. It
would be a very low-key thing, like
acoustic Beach Boys stuff, Elvis,
Chris Isaak. People usually think
your career is over when you record
a covers album or a Christmas

album. But my musician friends and I are always playing covers. We could probably do that album in a week." [224]

# - LANA DEL REY

*Summertime The Gershwin Version* by George Gershwin was released, assumed by many as the first single. Using the song, Lana directed attention to a fundraiser for struggling artists during the COVID-19 pandemic.

Other possible covers included *Take Me Home, Country Roads* by John Denver, a Harry Nilsson song, and *On Eagles' Wings* (previously released).

Talk of this album soon faded, and fans believe the project to be scrapped.

# PART ELEVEN
# CHEMTRAILS OVER THE COUNTRY CLUB/BLUE BANISTERS ERA

# 11.1.
# ALBUM: CHEMTRAILS OVER THE COUNTRY CLUB (2021)

# CHEMTRAILS OVER THE COUNTRY CLUB (2021)

## 1. White Dress
*(co-written with Jack Antonoff, third single)*

## 2. Chemtrails Over the Country Club
*(co-written with Jack Antonoff, second single)*

## 3. Tulsa Jesus Freak
*(co-written with Jack Antonoff, fourth single)*

## 4. Let Me Love You like a Woman
*(co-written with Jack Antonoff, first single)*

## 5. Wild at Heart
*(co-written with Jack Antonoff)*

## 6. Dark But Just a Game
*(co-written with Jack Antonoff)*

## 7. Not All Who Wander Are Lost
*(co-written with Jack Antonoff)*

## 8. Yosemite
*(co-written with Rick Nowels)*

## 9. Breaking Up Slowly
*(co-written and featuring Nikki Lane)*

## 10. Dance Till We Die
*(co-written with Jack Antonoff)*

## 11. For Free
*(Joni Mitchell cover, featuring Weyes Blood & Zella Day)*

## TOTAL RUNTIME: 45:28

*"I'm really excited right now. I don't want to take a break."* [225]

## - LANA DEL REY

Originally announced as *White Hot Forever*, Lana's seventh studio album, *Chemtrails Over the Country Club*, was released on March 19, 2021, through Interscope and Polydor records. The initial release date was postponed due to vinyl manufacturing delays.

*"Chemtrails Over the Country Club, right [...] 16-week delay on the vinyl process [...] because I can't get the record plants to open until March 5 [...] I was stressed out when I found out about the production taking 16 to 17 weeks. It is what it is, but in the mean time, I have some Patsy Cline songs I've been wanting to cover for a long time, and some Americana songs I've done with Nikki Lane."* [226]

## - LANA DEL REY

Production was handled by *Norman Fucking Rockwell!* mastermind, Jack Antonoff, but also included her most favourite collaborator, Rick Nowels. It was recorded in Conway Studios (Los Angeles) and Electric Lady (New York City). This album marks her second after *Lust For Life* to feature guest artists, namely Zella Day, Weyes Blood and Nikki Lane.

For many, *Chemtrails Over the Country Club* was an audio continuation from *Norman Fucking Rockwell!* (I mean, Jack Antonoff, am I right?), described as Americana and country folk. Lana highlighted some of her inspirations as star signs, her friends, her family, and the double standards felt by women in the music industry, stating she was *"sure there will be tinges of what I've been pondering in my new album"*.

"It makes me anxious listening to it, because I know it's going to be a hard road to get to where I want to be, to do what I want to do. A lot of that's going to involve writing classes and being uncomfortable in new places with not many friends, and raising my dogs and my cats and my chickens alone. It's going to be work. I hear Chemtrails and I think 'work' but I also think of my stunning girlfriends, who so much of the album *is about, and my beautiful siblings. Chemtrails is the title track because it mentions them all and it mentions wanting so much to be normal and realising that when you have an overactive, eccentric mind, a record like Chemtrails is just what you're going to get."* [227]

# - LANA DEL REY

Much like *Norman Fucking Rockwell!*, critics held the album in high esteem. The record received full marks from the Los Angeles Times (*"What's inarguable is that she's become one of the finest songwriters of her generation"*), The Telegraph (*"There is not a weak song or throwaway performance here, amidst many that only reveal their secrets on repeated listening"*), The Independent (*"A great storyteller, Del Rey consistently delivers the who, what, where and when"*), and NME (*"Lana Del Rey is at the peak of her game"*).

On that token, most publications felt it was slightly lesser impressive than the predecessor, such as Rolling Stone (*"it may not have as many grandiose showpieces as its older sibling"*, 80), Under The Radar (*"it isn't the universal smash hit that Norman F\*\*king Rockwell instantly was"*, 80), and DIY Magazine (*"An elegiac, introverted release that feels more like a late-career meditation than the victory lap for NFR!"* , 70). Sputnikmusic was particularly disappointed with a 30 score, stating *"If Norman Fucking Rockwell! was the record her non-partisan sympathisers dreamed she might make, this is the one they feared. It's hushed but impersonal, pared-back without having anything to reveal, and verbose without saying anything of substance"*. Still, the 81 overall Metacritic score is no failure, holding fort as her second-highest number to date.

The end-of-year articles spoke for themselves, with *Chemtrails Over the Country Club* hitting the top 10 on lists from The New York Times (7), Los Angeles Times (5), The Times (4), Slant (4), Mojo (3), and The Telegraph (2).

With 75,000 units sold, it debuted at number two on the US Billboard 200 chart, blocked by Justin Bieber's *Justice*. Regardless, it marked Lana's seventh top-ten debut on that chart. In the UK, *Chemtrails Over the Country Club* sold 40,000 copies, more than the rest of the top 10 combined, reaching number one, her fifth time to do so there. Other towering positions were reached in Argentina (6), Australia (2), Austria (4), Belgium (2), Canada (5), the Czech Republic (5), Denmark (2), Finalnd (5), France (3), Germany (3), Greece (3), Ireland (2), Italy (7), Lithuania (4), New Zealand (2), Norway (3), Poland (1), Portugal (1), Scotland (1), Spain (4), Sweden (3), and Switzerland (1).

"[It was the] first album where I knew what I wanted it to be, but I didn't know if I got there [...] it feels very much like when you're reaching in a relationship, when you're beckoning it like, ugh, I just want it so bad!" [228]

## - LANA DEL REY

## THE CHEMTRAILS ARTWORK UPSET PEOPLE

The album cover was shot by brother Charlie Grant for a change, and featured Lana surrounded by ten seemingly-white women. This non-inclusive image caused backlash, but Lana stood her ground, claiming that some of the ladies *were* of colour, the desaturated hue simply made it difficult to decipher.

"This was not intended—these are my best friends, since you are asking today. And damn! As it happens when it comes to my amazing friends and this cover, yes, there are people of colour on this records picture, and that's all I'll say about that, but thank you." [229]

## - LANA DEL REY

*"These are my friends, this is my life. We are all a beautiful mix of everything—some more than others which is visible and celebrated in everything I do. In 11 years working, I have always been extremely inclusive without even trying to. My best friends are rappers, my boyfriends have been rappers. My dearest friends have been from all over the place, so before you make comments again about a WOC POC issue, I'm not the one storming the capital, I'm literally changing the world by putting my life and thoughts and love out there on the table 24-7. Respect it."* [230]

# - LANA DEL REY

Her statement deepened her hole. Where she appeared to equate "rapper" with a person of colour was specifically criticised as problematic. She deleted the comments soon after.

"A woman still can't get mad, right?
Even when a mob mentality tries to
*incite*." [231]

# - LANA DEL REY

## CHEMTRAILS OVER THE COUNTRY CLUB SINGLES

Released on October 16, 2020, *Let Me Love You like a Woman* was *Chemtrails'* lead single. Critical feedback was warm, but some were wary of familiarity, such as Pitchfork, who said the song *"does not foretell a new direction"* for Del Rey. The track charted at 6 in Belgium and 9 in New Zealand. Interestingly, this song was written way back in consideration for *Ultraviolence*, only finding a home now.

The music video was released on the same day, filmed by Del Rey on her phone. Here, a natural-looking Lana sings to the camera intercut with footage of her performing live on tour (including with Joan Baez) and hanging out with her friends and family.

The title track for *Chemtrails over the Country Club* was the second single, released on January 11, 2021. Response was more favourable for this choice. Pitchfork was very fond of the concept, stating *"the title's flawless alignment with the mood and mien of that moment—the conspiracy-mindedness, the radiant gloom, the fragility, and the suggestion of the type of person associated with the words 'country club'— was an act of poetry. It* was remarkable to hear the bard of white American malaise sug-gest which delusion was gripping the nation". GigList observed, "Where Norman Fucking Rockwell! sounded like a dying bugle call for the American Dream, Chemtrails over the Country Club feels like Del Rey now wants to desperately clutch on to that for-gotten world of innocence, suburbia, and naivety". Vulture were less enthusiastic, feeling the song *"doesn't have much profound to say"*. Regardless, it charted fairly well, reaching 5 in Bel-gium, 10 in Greece, 8 in Lithuania, and 4 in Sweden.

The intense music video was released the same day. Di-rected by film production duo BRTHR, Mina Takavoli from Pitchfork described the clip as: *"Lana in a diamanté mesh mask, looking a little like Hedy Lamarr in low fidelity, glancing sweetly from the driver's seat of a mid-century Mercedes-Benz Cabriolet [while] chemtrails dart overhead in crosshatch as Lana stares up with widened eyes."*

Lana may or may not also turn into a werewolf with her friends near the end, which Rolling Stone described as *"stere-otypical Lana Del Rey"*.

*White Dress* was the official third single, released on March 26, 2021.

"What I like about that song is that for all of its weirdness, when you get to the end of it, you understand exactly what it's about. I hate when I hear a song that has a great melody, but I have no idea what they're talking about. In the grunge movement, a lot of the lyrics were super abstract, but the melodies and the tonality were such a vibe that you felt like you knew exactly what the singer was thinking. Nowadays, you get a beautiful melody, but you don't really know what the person is talking about, or if it's even important to them." [232]

# - LANA DEL REY

The music video premiered on March 20, 2021. Directed by Constellation Jones, the clip was intended to show Lana roller skating around a desert scene, but she could not fulfil the brief due to an elbow injury. Instead, Ganna Bogdan played the role as her body double.

"When you see my second video for this album, don't think that the fact I'm wearing a cast is symbolic for

anything other than thinking I was
still a pro figure skater. I wiped out
on my beautiful skates before the
video even began after a long day of
figure eights and jumps in the twilight
of the dezert [sic]." [233]

# - LANA DEL REY

*Tulsa Jesus Freak* was the fourth and final *Chemtrails* single, released on March 26, 2021, the same day as *White Dress*. No official video was gifted to our streaming services.

## OTHER NOTEWORTHY SONGS FROM CHEMTRAILS OVER THE COUNTRY CLUB

The inspiration for *Dark But Just a Game* came from a party hosted by Madonna and Guy Oseary, where St. Vincent and Jack Antonoff were in attendance.

"Something happened, kind of like a
situation—never meet your idols. And
I just thought, 'I think it's interesting
that the best musicians end up in
such terrible places'. I thought to

myself, 'I'm going to try my best not
to change because I love who I am'. I
said, 'Jack, it's dark'. And he said,
'Well, it's dark— but it's just a game'." [234]

# - LANA DEL REY

Antonoff added:

"Dark But Just A Game is so her
to me. Fly down the rabbit hole and
smile in the same breath." [235]

# - JACK ANTONOFF

*Not All Who Wander Are Lost* was originally recorded for *Norman Fucking Rockwell!*. The version on *Chemtrails over the Country Club* was that exact recording without any alterations.

Fans will remember *Yosemite* as an outtake from *Lust for Life*, removed because *"it was just too happy"*. It is finally with us, thanks to *Chemtrails*.

"I kinda want to dig into a little
bit more of the acoustic side of the
record... like I have a track called

Yosemite which I really like—which is just a little more laid back, kind of a love song that I did all in one take in the room." [236]

# - LANA DEL REY

*Breaking Up Slowly* featured Nikki Lane. The session blatantly went well, because Del Rey and Lane announced a joint album soon following.

"I obviously want her to be able to have control with the way her art plays out. But knowing that we're working together on these projects, I was like, 'What are we gonna do with that other song?' And she's like, 'Well, we're gonna do more!' She wants to lean in. Her voice naturally works so well in that country space. And I think what you've seen with Lana, with her records across her career, is that she likes to lean into all *of those characters, or all of those different genres, different producers that she's worked with, and sounds that she's worked with. So I think she wants to lean into country, and I love that. We've been writing songs driving around in an F-150 in Texas. I think you can expect to see the fruit of that."* [237]

# - NIKKI LANE

Based on the lack of news, many hypothesise this project to be shelved.

*Dance Till We Die* features the cheeky lyric, *"I'm coverin' Joni and dancin' with Joan, Stevie's callin' on the telephone"*. These legendary namedrops check out, Lana having performed with Joan Baez live, collaborated with Stevie Nicks on *Beautiful People Beautiful Problems* (*Lust For Life*) and covering Joni Mitchell on the very next track.

*For Free* is the aforementioned Joni Mitchell cover, featuring Weyes Blood and Zella Day. The original can be found on Joni's 1970 record *Ladies of the Canyon*.

## CHEMTRAILS OVER THE COUNTRY CLUB
## UNRELEASED OUTTAKES

Reports state that *Yes To Heaven* was considered but rejected for this album (the fourth or even fifth time this has happened).

Due to the close recording sessions between *Chemtrails Over the Country Club* and her next record, *Blue Banisters*, many tracks crossed over. This includes *Black Bathing* Suit and, more notably, *Dealer*, the scrapped song from the ill-fated The Last Shadow Puppets collaboration.

*Loved You Then and Now* appeared on the original *Chemtrails Over the Country Club* tracklist but was then pushed back to feature on *Blue Banisters*, but did not materialise there either. There are no reported leaks at this time.

# 11.2.
# QUITTING SOCIAL MEDIA
# (SORTA)

In September 2021, Lana announced her decision to deactivate her social media life, most likely after the onslaught of negative press concerning her COVID mask, the artwork for *Chemtrails*, and the Ann Powers dispute. But she assured fans that the work would continue.

*"I want to say a heartfelt thank you for continuing to see me through the music. It's always important to be witnessed. Right now, I think I'm going to keep my circle a little bit closer*

*and continue to develop some other skills and interests."* [238]

# - LANA DEL REY

At the publication date of this book, Lana has reactivated her Instagram @Honeymoon, but she's set it to private. She and the other Grant siblings can be followed on TikTok via @familyheirlooms. In Januray 2023, an Insta account @oceanblvd appeared and was verified, instantly followed by Del Rey's managers. There is a good chance this is an official Lana profile to promote the new record.

# 11.3.
# ALBUM: BLUE BANISTERS
# (2021)

# BLUE BANISTERS (2021)

## 1. Text Book
*(co-written with Gabe Simon, promotional single)*

## 2. Blue Banisters
*(co-written with Gabe Simon, first single)*

## 3. Arcadia
*(co-written with Drew Erickson, second single)*

## 4. Interlude - The Trio
*(written by Ennio Morricone)*

## 5. Black Bathing Suit
*(co-written with Drew Erickson and Zachary Dawes)*

## 6. If You Lie Down with Me
*(co-written with Drew Erickson and Barrie-James O'Neill)*

## 7. Beautiful
*(co-written with Drew Erickson)*

## 8. Violets for Roses
*(co-written with Drew Erickson)*

## 9. Dealer
*(featuring Miles Kane (uncredited), co-written with Loren Humphrey, Miles Kane, Tyler Parkford, and Zachary Dawes)*

## 10. Thunder
*(co-written with Zachary Dawes)*

## 11. Wildflower Wildfire
*(co-written with Mike Dean, Sean Solymar, and Sage Skolfield, promotional single)*

## 12. Nectar of the Gods
*(co-written Barrie-James O'Neill)*

## 13. Living Legend
*(co-written Barrie-James O'Neill)*
## 14. Cherry Blossom
*(co-written Rick Nowels)*
## 15. Sweet Carolina
*(co-written Alana Champion, Caroline Grant, and Robert Grant Jr.)*

### TOTAL RUNTIME: 61:54

*"It's a compilation of older songs and a few newer songs, some written by family and friends and mostly old collaborators."* [238]

# - LANA DEL REY

Four days before the release of *Chemtrails Over the Country Club*, Lana announced her eighth studio album, originally titled *Rock Candy Sweet*. Said announcement was in response to Harper's Bazaar article *Lana Del Rey Can't Qualify Her Way Out Of Being Held Accountable* with:

*"Just want to say thank you again for the kind articles like this one and for reminding me that my career was built on cultural appropriation*

*and glamorising domestic abuse. I will continue to challenge those thoughts on my next record June I titled Rock Candy Sweet.*" [239]

# - LANA DEL REY

Seven months later (October 22, 2021), her second album of the year arrived, except with a brand new title: *Blue Banisters*. Released through Interscope and Polydor Records, the production team was extensive, featuring (but not limited to) usual suspects such as Zachary Dawes, Loren Humphrey, Mike Dean, Barrie-James O'Neill, and Rick Nowels. It was recorded at Conway Recording Studios (Los Angeles), Dean's List House of Hits (Texas), Punto Rec Studios (Turin), and TaP Studios (London). The artwork was shot by Neil Krug, where Lana sits flanked by her doggos, Tex and Mex.

In many ways, *Blue Banisters* could be argued as the *"collection of unreleased songs"* compilation that Lana was forever threatening to release. Point proven when, despite being recorded so close to *Chemtrails*, the sound here was slightly different, with more jazzy undertones beneath her standard folky poppy Americana (and even includes a bass-heavy trap beat on *Interlude - The Trio*). Theme-wise, A.V. Club called it a *"breakup record"*.

Even the most antagonistic of critics (with a 60 score, The Guardian used the word *"samey-ness"*) were impressed with the quantity and quality of Lana's output this year. Variety said *Blue Banisters "offers a rare glimpse of an artist securing her legacy, one song at a time"* giving it 82. Rolling Stone called it *"pure"* (80), Spin called it *"present"* (80), and Pitchfork called it *"rewarding"* (77), while The Independent claimed it *"far more elliptical and mysterious than it first appears"* (80). With an overall 80 Metacritic score, it's her third highest, only one point below *Chemtrails Over the Country Club*. It was Spin's 3rd and The Sunday Times' 10th best record of the year, respectively.

With 33,000 sales, *Blue Banisters* debuted at number 8 on the Billboard 200, her 8th to hit that top 10, but her first to miss the top 3 since her *Lana Del Ray* debut. Other top 10 charting positions took place in Argentina (1), Australia (3), Austria (8), Belgium (4), Canada (10), Denmark (1), France (7), Germany (6), Greece (8), Ireland (4), Lithuania (8), New Zealand (8), Poland (4), Portugal (3), Scotland (3), Spain (7), Switzerland (6), and the UK (2). Furthermore, *Blue Banisters* set a record for Lana, making her the act with the most number-one albums on Billboard's Alternative Albums chart ever.

*Blue Banisters was more of an explanatory album, more of a defensive album, which is why I didn't promote it, period, at all. I didn't want anyone to listen to it. I just wanted it to be there in case anyone was ever curious for any information."* [240]

# - LANA DEL REY

## BLUE BANISTERS SINGLES

On May 20, 2021, three singles dropped simultaneously. The first two, *Text Book* and *Wildflower Wildfire*, were promotional only. Meanwhile, the *Blue Banisters* title track received a far more official release.

That included a music video weirdly surfacing five months later, on October 20, 2021. Chris Ripley filmed the clip, which features Lana, her sister Chuck, and her friends fittingly painting bannisters blue. They also bake later.

*Arcadia* was released as the second and final single on September 8, 2021. Lana has called it her favourite song on the album, informing us that it originated as a poem.

*"They built me up three hundred feet
tall just to tear me down,
So I'm leavin' with nothing but
laughter, and this town, Arcadia,
Findin' my way to ya,
I'm leavin' them as I was, five foot
eight,
Western bound, plus the hate that
they gave,
By the way, thanks for that, on the*

*way, I'll pray for ya,*
*But you'll need a miracle,*
*America."*

# - LANA DEL REY

(LYRICS FROM *ARCADIA*)

Universal acclaimed for the song followed. Spin observed it as an *"astonishing farewell to an industry that trashed [Del Rey] from the beginning"*, while NPR bowed to the lyrics that *"carefully construct the very landscapes she describes"*.

Released on October 7, 2021, the music video was directed by "nobody" according to Lana, although she thanked her sister, brother, and Chris Ripley for their camera work. Here we see Lana singing, as city space footage is projected onto her body. An alternate one-shot music video exists too.

## OTHER NOTEWORTHY SONGS FROM BLUE BANISTERS

*I*nterlude - *The Trio* samples a piece of music from the 1966 film *The Good, the Bad and the Ugly* by Ennio Morricone.

When Lana posted a screenshot of her voice memo app to Instagram in 2020, fans noticed two songs called *Grenadine quarantine 2* and *If this is the end ...I want a boyfriend*, leading to speculation that they would appear on *Chemtrails Over the Country Club*, but they never did. Instead, these both turned out to be working titles for *Black Bathing Suit*.

As previously discussed, *Blue Banisters* largely served

as an outtake dumping ground. For example, many unused songs recorded for *Ultraviolence* ended up here, such as *Cherry Blossom, Nectar of the Gods, Living Legend,* and *If You Lie Down with Me.* Similarly, two songs from the scrapped collaborative album with The Last Shadow Puppets can be found on this record too, namely *Dealer* and *Thunder.*

*"I think I need to add that song Dealer, where I'm just screaming my head off. People don't know what it sounds like when I yell, and I do yell."* [241]

## - LANA DEL REY

The closing song *Sweet Carolina* is extra special, as it was co-written with her father and sister, Rob and Chuck Grant, along with Alana Champion. Reportedly, it took them 20 minutes to finish, with the excellent cryptocurrency lyric taken from a private conversation between Champion and Chuck.

*You name your babe Lilac Heaven,
After your iPhone 11.
'Crypto forever!' screams your stupid boyfriend.*

*Fuck you, Kevin."*

# - LANA DEL REY

(LYRICS FROM *SWEET CAROLINA*)

## BLUE BANISTERS UNRELEASED OUTTAKES

Originally written for *Ultraviolence*, *Fine China* was considered for *Blue Banisters* too but ultimately did not fit the team. A 2016 version leaked in 2017.

Some claim another *Ultraviolence* outtake *Wild One* was given a shot but missed *Blue Banisters* too, which had also happened with *Honeymoon*. The 2012 and 2015 versions leaked in 2021.

*Loved You Then and Now* was intended for *Chemtrails Over the Country Club* but was reconsidered for this album, failing again. The original title for this song was the same as the one considered for this record, namely *Rock Candy Sweet*.

*The Big Eyes* soundtrack song *I Can Fly* was seen on earlier tracklistings for this record.

# 11.4.
# RELATIONSHIP STATUS: SEAN LARKIN AND CLAYTON JOHNSON (PLUS A GENERAL CATCHUP)

Several men were rumoured to be in Lana's life over the recent years, including rapper G-Eazy (2017) and Chase Stogel (2019). Policeman and reality TV star Sean "Sticks" Larkin dated Lana from 2019 - 2020, but they broke up, announced by Larkin himself.

*"When Sean and I broke up, I just thought it was the end of the world."* [242]

## - LANA DEL REY

Musician Clayton Johnson was a far more significant human in Lana's life. It has been said the couple met on the dating app Bumble, and by December 2020, chatter circulated that they were engaged, especially after Lana was seen wearing a ring on The Tonight Show Starring Jimmy Fallon.

Johnson's presence can be felt all throughout *Blue Banisters*, where he provided production to *Interlude - The Trio*. Additionally, the song *Text Book* is said to be about him. He initially played a starring role in the video for the *Blue Banisters* title track, but was cut from the final edit, presumably because the two had split by then, confirmed in mid-2021.

# 11.5.
# STOLEN POETRY

Lana's second poetry book, *Behind the Iron Gates - Insights from an Institution*, was announced as far back as 2020, with the poem *Patent Leather Do-Over* shared to Instagram on May 23 of that year. Unfortunately, in 2022, her car was burgled and she lost a laptop full of unfinished songs and the 200-page manuscript of the book, her only working copy.

"A few months ago, I parked my car on Melrose Place and I stepped away for a minute. The one time I left my backpack inside my car, someone broke all of the windows and took it." [243]

## - LANA DEL REY

She remotely wiped the laptop but it was not backed up on a cloud, possibly due to Lana's past troubles with leaks.

*"Despite all of this happening, I am confident in the record to come, and despite so many safety factors in so many different levels, I really want to persist and make the best art I can."* [244]

## - LANA DEL REY

# 11.6.
# 2022 SIDEQUESTS: EUPHORIA, FATHER JOHN MISTY, AND TAYLOR SWIFT

The Queen of Soundtracks blessed us mere mortals with another, this time for the television series *Euphoria*. Co-written with Nasri and titled *Watercolor Eyes*, it premiered on January 21, 2022.

Moving into June, and Father John Mistry released his single for *Buddy's Rendezvous*. Rather than simply giving fans the album version, we were treated to a Lana cover as well.

Then, on October 21, 2022, Taylor Swift's tenth studio album, *Midnights*, came along and utterly shattered every 2022 world records. The fourth track, *Snow on the Beach*, was co-written by Lana as well as with Jack Antonoff. Lyrically about *"falling in love with someone at the same time as they're falling in love with you"* (according to Swift), the song proved to be a huge hit, debuting at number 4 on the Billboard Hot 100, Lana's highest-peaking entry on that chart thanks to that additional Swifty power. Boasting over 15 million Spotify streams in its first 24 hours, it holds the record for the biggest opening day for a female collaboration.

*"She was very adamant that she wanted me to be on the album, and I really liked that song. I thought it was nice to be able to bridge that world, since Jack [Antonoff] and I work together and so do Jack and Taylor."* [245]

# - LANA DEL REY

In later interviews, Lana expressed some regret over how little vocals she contributed, especially because Taylor had asked for more.

*"Well, first of all, I had no idea I was the only feature [on that song]. Had I known, I would have sung the entire second verse like she wanted. My job as a feature on a big artist's album is to make sure I help add to the production*

of the song, so I was more focused on the production." [245]

# - LANA DEL REY

# PART TWELVE
# DID YOU KNOW THAT THERE'S A TUNNEL UNDER OCEAN BLVD ERA

# 11.4.
# ALBUM: DID YOU KNOW THAT THERE'S A TUNNEL UNDER OCEAN BLVD (2023)

# DID YOU KNOW THAT THERE'S A TUNNEL UNDER OCEAN BLVD (2023)

1. The Grants

*(co-written with Mike Hermosa, third single)*

2. Did You Know That There's a Tunnel Under Ocean Blvd

*(co-written with Mike Hermosa, first single)*

3. Sweet

4. A&W

*(co-written with Jack Antonoff, second single)*

5. Judah Smith Interlude

6. Candy Necklace

*(featuring Jon Batiste)*

7. Jon Batiste Interlude

8. Kintsugi

9. Fingertips

10. Paris, Texas

*(featuring SYML)*

11. Grandfather Please Stand on the Shoulders of My Father While He's Deep-Sea Fishing

*(featuring Riopy)*

12. Let the Light In (featuring Father John Misty)

*(featuring Father John Misty)*

13. Margaret

*(featuring Bleachers)*

14. Fishtail

15. Peppers

*(featuring Tommy Genesis)*

16. Taco Truck x VB

TOTAL RUNTIME: 77:45

"Family of origin is the overall theme.
I think with Blue Banisters, I wanted
to capture this idea too, but I flew
it under the radar. I was trying to
address some criticisms that I had
heard said after Chemtrails. Mostly
that people don't know much about
me. I didn't promote that theme of
Blue Banisters at all intentionally. In
this album, I got to really finish my
thoughts and get super specific, which
I was not comfortable with completely
before. I do list my grandpa, my
brother, my dad, my Uncle Dave." [247]

# - LANA DEL REY

Released through Interscope and Polydor Records on March 24, 2023, *Did you know that there's a tunnel under Ocean Blvd* is Lana's ninth and (at the time of this publication) most recent studio album. The list of producers seems mostly familiar (Jack Antonoff, Mike Hermosa, Drew Erickson, Zach Dawes, and Benji), but it is Lana's first record since her *Lana Del Ray* debut not to receive any help from Rick Nowels. *Did you know...* is another one of Lana's collaboration-heavy offerings, featuring the likes of Jon Batiste, Bleachers, Father John Misty, Tommy Genesis, SYML, and Riopy.

The title is quite literal, inspired by a closed tunnel under the Jergins Trust Building in Long Beach, California.

"I was spending a lot of time in Long Beach, and I had read that there was a tunnel sealed up under the Jergins [Trust] Building. All of the mosaic ceilings were still perfectly preserved, but no one could get in. I had also been listening to a lot of Harry Nilsson. He has this song called 'Don't Forget Me'. That sentiment, plus this man-made tunnel that was sealed up but was so beautiful, I liked the idea of putting them together. I knew right off the bat that was going to be the title." [246]

## - LANA DEL REY

Lana confessed that the lengthy title was almost even longer:

*Did You Know That There's a Tunnel Under Ocean Blvd Pearl Watch Me on Ring a Bell Psycho Lifeguard.*

"[Neil Krug] mocked it up, but we realised that maybe it was a bit much to have six titles in one. Then, he was like, 'This is reminding me of a format that I've always wanted to play with. What if we just used one title, but then we filled the rest of the page with everyone who's featured and everyone who engineered it?' He mocked that up on the portrait shot, and I was like, 'You did it'. That was a really psychotic day because I was like, 'Am I willing to literally burn everything down to the ground by having some strange, nonsensical title?'" [246]

# - LANA DEL REY

Speaking of Neil Krug, he shot the album cover like he has done several times before (such as with *Ultraviolence* and *Blue Banisters*). Lana announced an alternate version of the artwork in which she was partially topless, but ultimately decided against it.

*"My original cover was nude, then I thought about it, and I was like, maybe not right now, because there are some other things I want to do where I feel like that could get in the way. For each shot, we were really specific about the idea and the mood. He took 65 shots in a row, and we used every single one of them, because I told him I didn't want him to just shoot, shoot, shoot, I wanted to take my time and think about what I wanted to express in my face."* [246]

## - LANA DEL REY

*"I might not have used [the nude shot], but there's definitely something there. The idea behind it was, instead of*

being exposed for things that weren't true, I wanted to reveal something about myself that I actually thought was beautiful, but in the end, I got nervous about doing that because I was like, 'is this an artistic inspiration that came to me or is this a reaction to something I feel is critical about me?' I never liked to do anything in response to something that's fear-based or based on what people think about me [...] But the good thing is that the songs are so wordy that if you listen to them carefully, they're revealing in the same way the photo would've been. I was like, 'OK, I'll let the songs do the talking for now." [246]

# - LANA DEL REY

At the end of December, Lana promoted the album with one singular billboard, hilariously erected in Tulsa, the hometown of her ex, Sean Larkin.

Soundwise, Lana has described the record as *"spiritual"* with a stream-of-consciousness style of lyrical delivery.

*"It's more just like: I'm angry. The songs are very conversational. For the first song, I pressed record and sang, 'When I look back, tracing fingertips over plastic bags, I think I wish I could extrapolate some small intention or maybe get your attention for a minute or two.' It's a very wordy album. So there's no room for colour. It's almost like I'm typing in my mind.* [248]

## - LANA DEL REY

### DID YOU KNOW THAT THERE'S A TUNNEL UNDER OCEAN BLVD SINGLES

The first single was the title track, melting its soft chamber pop into our collective ears on December 7, 2022. Everybody loved it, with Pitchfork noting the *"slow, dreamy ballad"* was loaded with the *"incidental moments that interest Lana now"*. In a Billboard poll, 80% of music fans called it the best song of the week.

The second single, *A&W*, was released on Valentine's Day 2023 and caused a much bigger whirlpool of attention. Standing for *"American Whore"*, it is essentially two songs in one: the first half, a folky ballad, and the second, a hip-hoppy trap piece referencing the *Down Down Baby* nursery rhyme. Rolling Stone said it was *"classic Lana in every way imaginable"* while Pitchfork slapped that yummy Best New Track sticker on top while loving it as a *"psychedelic, collagist freakout"*. Other publications noted its hard-hitting lyrics concerning rape culture: *"If I told you that I was raped, do you really think that anybody would think I didn't ask for it? I didn't ask for it. I won't testify, I already fucked up my story"*.

"Can't wait for everyone to hear this album. American Whore is my favourite we've ever done." [249]

# - JACK ANTONOFF

The album's opening song, *The Grants* functions as the album's third single (released on March 14, 2023). With a clear gospel influence, its title and lyrical content are obvious references to Lana's family, just like she promised.

"My sister's first-born child, I'm gonna take that too with me.
My grandmother's last smile, I'm gonna

take that too with me.
It's a beautiful life. Remember that
too for me."

# - LANA DEL REY

(LYRICS FROM *THE GRANTS*)

## OTHER NOTEWORTHY SONGS FROM DID YOU KNOW THAT THERE'S A TUNNEL UNDER OCEAN BLVD

*Margaret* features Bleachers (aka Jack Antonoff) and was inspired by Antonoff's fiancé, actress Margaret Qualley.

Fans were quick to note the *VB* in *Taco Truck x VB* meant a new version of 2018's *Venice Bitch* would be closing the album.

# 12.2.
# LANA'S DADDY'S ALBUM

What initially sounded like a joke turned out to be entirely true: Lana's father, Rob Grant, has a debut album named *Lost at Sea*. With a mid-2023 release, one might be worried he's trying to steal sales away from Lana's *Did You Know That There's a Tunnel Under Ocean Blvd*, but she seems unconcerned, instead contributing her voice to the title track and the song *Hollywood Bowl*.

*"I mean, let's get real. He's always been the star."* [250]

## - LANA DEL REY

# 12.3.
# RELATIONSHIP STATUS: MIKE HERMOSA AND JACK DONOGHUE

If there is a male face to *Did you know that there's a tunnel under Ocean Blvd* that would be her ex-boyfriend, cameraman Mike Hermosa. Hermosa would often strum his guitar in the presence of Lana, who would sneakily record him and write lyrics to his creations. Five of those pieces ended on the album.

"When we broke up, I was like, 'You know at some point we're going to have to talk about the fact that you have half of this album. It will come out [...] He's definitely warmed-

*up to it. He has to be, he's on the album sleeve!"* [251]

# - LANA DEL REY

Based on many Instagram photos, it appears that Lana has been dating musician Jack Donoghue since mid-2022. While his fame is but a speck compared to Lana's, Jack's music groups (Salem and Young Cream) are semi-well known in industry circles, the man even boasting a credit on Kanye West's 2013 song *Black Skinhead* from *Yeezus*.

# 12.4.
# THE GREATEST AMERICAN SONGWRITER OF THE 21ST CENTURY

"No matter what happens from here on out, I already learned everything. I can tell, I've learned everything I need to know, I don't need to experience anything else. I'm just really happy that I pushed through all those turbulent times that were sometimes brought upon by myself and sometimes were suppressed onto me by other people and things, to the point that

I'm just so lucky that my heart isn't fragmented all over the world, bits of it with other people who it doesn't belong to, that my head is clear enough to not have my self-will run riot all the time." [250]

# - LANA DEL REY

The declaration of Lana's genius is no surprise to long-serving fans, but it is only in these later years that the critical world has caught up. In 2020, Del Rey was the only musician featured on The Washington Post's *Decade of Influence* list. In 2023, Rolling Stone dubbed her *"the greatest American songwriter of the 21st century"*. And, also in 2023, Billboard awarded her with their acclaimed Visionary Award.

"I think the word 'visionary' could have been exchanged with any word when you're up here. But if you were wondering, for my fans, I don't exactly have a long-term vision, at all. But if you were curious, I am very, very happy [...] When I released my first album 14 years ago, the waters were not quite as warm. So I'm really happy for everyone who feels like it's a wonderful time in the culture to be themselves and to express themselves. It didn't feel that way in 2008, and I'm so grateful to be in the best company I've ever been in. Thank you. I feel like being happy is the ultimate. So I did it. Thank you, Billboard." [252]

## - LANA DEL REY

# 12.5.
# LANA'S CONCLUDING IMPACT

"I think if you're a singer and people's opinions of the work change so many times, you kind of realise: OK, there's something to be learned from what you hear. At the same time, I'm definitely not one who thrives from outside validation, other than from a few people. It was very important to me to not have any influence from the outside culture that didn't

resonate with me. I always knew
that I was going to do something else
as well, aside from singing. To be more
connected to what that path was
going to be, I just needed to tune in
more to my gut." [250]

# - LANA DEL REY

E ver since Lana discovered her ability to translate thoughts into art, she has never shown any indication of slowing down. But for us sideline admirers, her near-two-decade career zoomed so quickly past that now may be a good time to pause and reflect.

So, how does one measure success? Is it sales? With over 20 million albums shipped in the United States and United Kingdom alone, she's got that. Is it charting positions? Her albums and singles have hit number one in almost every country imaginable, not to mention her four billion+ video streams on YouTube/Vevo. Is it awards? Del Rey has 2 Brit Awards, 2 MTV Europe Music Awards, a Satellite Award and 9 GAFFA Awards, along with nominations for 6 Grammys and a Golden Globe Award.

But, like every legendary tale, Lana's true legacy will live through the artists she has inspired along the way.

"She created us." [253]

## - BILLIE EILISH

"Lana Del Rey is simply one of America's greatest songwriters." [254]

## - BRUCE SPRINGSTEEN

"Lana and Kurt are the only two true musical geniuses I've ever known. And by that, I mean they can Spielberg anything." [255]

## - COURTNEY LOVE

"Lana Del Rey, in my opinion, is one of the best musical artists ever." [256]

## - TAYLOR SWIFT

"Mystique is your greatest asset, because you don't want people to

Know too much. You have what Prince had." [257]

## - ELTON JOHN

"I am a Lana fangirl." [258]

## -ADELE

"You can take all the crack songwriters and put them in a bunker for a thousand years, and they would not come up with 'Fucked My Way Up To The Top' ever, which I think will go down as the greatest song title of all time." [259]

## - FATHER JOHN MISTY

"It's all about how you feel, not about what other people think." [260]

## - LANA DEL REY

The attacks on Lana lasted many stormy years, as she was stomped upon by hostile boots and sliced with jagged names. But she refused to break until it was the world's perspective that broke. As we've shown, those critics and internet baddies bowed their heads in defeat, one by one. And within those moments of contemplative surrender, they finally met Lana on her melodious level.

Here, they found her petals were not so monochrome, while her ideals were not solely a messy tangle of masochistic self-destruction. Instead, a multicoloured radiance of love pulsates beneath the stem, endlessly stimulated by the faces around her, romantically seeking to absorb the most fascinating qualities in everything, then exuding that energy filtered through her particular brand of magic.

In the end, the saddest flower was not sad whatsoever. Rather, it provided the cure to sadness, conversing with the emotional vacancy everyone feels on occasion and then filling that emptiness with harmonious music. Like building blocks of motivation, Lana helps us to escape the monotony of melancholic loneliness until we reach a lush hill towering above former low points. And it is here that Lana sits wearing a knowing smirk, with only the initiated invited to her world, now understanding that each of our flowers can surrender into the joyful inspiration behind our darkness. Perhaps we can never be her, but we can use her to discover ourselves.

"Find someone who has a life that
you want and figure out how they got
it. Read books pick your role models
wisely, find out what they did
and do it." [260]

# - LANA DEL REY

# AUTHOR NOTE

Thank you for reading my book! I must tell you, this is a special publication, not only because I love Lana Del Rey, but because, at the end of 2022, I quit my job to dedicate myself as a full-time author. Eek!

Some people say I'm crazy. Others say I'm brave, which is probably a polite word for crazy. My dad said to write a best-selling book is a one-in-a-million chance. I told him I'd just have to write a million books then.

I'm not claiming that my Lana biography will skyrocket me to fame, but if it shoves a spoon of food into my mouth and allows me to pen my next project without worry, that would be the dream coming true right there! And that is where you come in.

Amazon's algorithm is an extremely intelligent beast that judges authors' products based on many factors. But inarguably, our most significant power comes from **verified reviews**. So when you take a few minutes to tell the world what you thought of this book, the website wakes up and lifts the title to higher eyes, feeding itself in the process. The author has no control over this side of the deal. It entirely relies on you!

Hence, please consider reviewing this Lana Del Rey biography and help me work another day. You wouldn't believe the difference a single rating makes, and I read every one of them.

Thank you again so very much!
Jared Woods

# F**ked
# My Way
# Up To
# The Top

THE COMPLETE BIOGRAPHY OF

# LANA DEL REY

USING HER OWN WORDS

# ABOUT THE AUTHOR

B orn in South Africa and now homeless as a nomadic something or other, Jared Woods does whatever he wants. His scriptwriting for the YouTube channel Pencilmation has been viewed by billions of people, with scripts surpassing the 100 million mark. An additional million-plus viewers have enjoyed his blog, Juice Nothing.

F\*\*ked My Way Up to the Top is Jared's first biography publication, but he is no stranger to music journalism, demonstrated by his guide *The 250 Best Albums of the Decade* (2019). His other publications include the fictional novel *This Is Your Brain On Drugs* (2016), and the self-help books *Heartbreak Sucks! How to Get Over Your Breakup in 30 Days* (2021) and *Swiping Right* released earlier this year. But most importantly, we have Jared's own religious scripture, the *Janthopoyism Bible* (2022). Get that first.

Further creative projects include his one-panel Instagram comic *#legobiscuits*, his solo music under the name *Coming Down Happy*, his "singing" for the band *Sectlinefor*, and his film production called *Definitely Not a Cry For Help* which is already partially on YouTube.

Support Jared on ***Patreon.com/legotrip***

Visit Jared at ***JaredWoodsSavedMyLife.com***

Follow Jared on Facebook, Instagram, and Twitter ***@legotrip***

## OTHER BOOKS BY JARED WOODS

Janthopoyism Bible (2022)

Swiping Right (2023)

Heartbreak Sucks! How to Get Over Your Breakup in 30 Days (2021)

The 250 Best Albums of the Decade (2010 - 2019) (2019)

This Is Your Brain On Drugs (2016)

# REFERENCES

1. *https://www.vanityfair.com/hollywood/2014/07/who-lana-del-rey-slept-with*
2. *https://www.complex.com/music/2013/05/lana-del-rey-says-people-disrespecting-her-music-makes-her-want-to-drink-again*
3. *https://www.youtube.com/watch?v=-7QwPDRP__o*
4. *https://enidnetwork.org/2021/03/01/lana-del-rey-and-the-dreams-of-a-generation/*
5. *https://www.complex.com/style/2014/10/lana-del-rey-interviews-her-sister-chuck-grant-about-photography*
6. *https://www.smh.com.au/entertainment/music/lolita-in-the-hood-20140505-37r6n.html*
7. *https://www.smh.com.au/entertainment/music/lolita-in-the-hood-20140505-37r6n.html*
8. *https://www.nme.com/news/music/lana-del-rey-198-1272601*
9. *https://www.nme.com/news/music/lana-del-rey-149-1264690*
10. *https://www.smh.com.au/entertainment/music/lolita-in-the-hood-20140505-37r6n.html*
11. *https://outofshell.tistory.com/m/625*
12. *https://www.smh.com.au/entertainment/music/lolita-in-the-hood-20140505-37r6n.html*
13. *https://www.pressparty.com/pg/newsdesk/londonnewsdesk/view/112592/?isworld=y*
14. *https://www.bbc.com/news/entertainment-arts-16729651*
15. *https://www.christianpost.com/news/lana-del-rey-opens-up-on-spirituality-and-beliefs.html*
16. *https://www.thelefortreport.com/blog/2011-09/lana-del-rey-take-me-to-the-marina/*
17. *https://essentialsmagazine.com.au/people/sombre-lust-for-lana/*
18. *https://www.clashmusic.com/features/american-dreamer-lana-del-rey-interviewed/*
19. *https://www.electronicbeats.net/lana-del-rey-interview/*
20. *https://www.distractify.com/p/lana-del-rey-religion*
21. *https://www.electronicbeats.net/lana-del-rey-interview/*
22. *https://www.vogue.co.uk/article/lana-del-rey*
23. *https://www.youtube.com/watch?v=uaQBSjTska4*
24. *https://faroutmagazine.co.uk/lana-del-rey-album-born-to-die-10-years/*

25. *https://www.songfacts.com/facts/lana-del-rey/millionaire-dollar-man*
26. *https://www.mtv.com/news/2nps55/lana-del-rey-first-album-5-points-records-interview*
27. *https://lizzygrant4ever.tumblr.com/post/60113849123/lizzy-grant-interviewed-by-mi-chael-mizrahi*
28. *https://junkee.com/lana-del-rey-doesnt-like-feminism-but-she-does-like-space/35463*
29. *https://pitchfork.com/features/rising/8657-lana-del-rey/*
30. *https://www.mtv.com/news/2nps55/lana-del-rey-first-album-5-points-records-interview*
31. *https://thequietus.com/articles/07106-lana-del-rey-interview*
32. *http://www.indexmagazine.com/interviews/Lizzy_grant2.shtml*
33. *https://www.huffpost.com/entry/interview-singersongwrite_b_159346*
34. *http://lanaboards.com/topic/2247-lana-del-rey-now-interview-with-princess-superstar-moi-je-joue-producer/*
35. *https://www.vice.com/en/article/8qbydz/interview-electroclash-firecracker-princess-super-star-gets-honest*
36. *https://www.electronicbeats.net/lana-del-rey-interview/*
37. *https://www.huffpost.com/entry/interview-singersongwrite_b_159346*
38. *https://thequietus.com/articles/07106-lana-del-rey-interview*
39. *https://www.cosmopolitan.com/uk/entertainment/news/a14848/lana-del-rey-explains-her-name-1/*
40. *https://www.mtv.com/news/2nps55/lana-del-rey-first-album-5-points-records-interview*
41. *https://www.bbc.com/news/entertainment-arts-16729651*
42. *https://www.mtv.com/news/2nps55/lana-del-rey-first-album-5-points-records-interview*
43. *https://www.undertheradarmag.com/news/lana_del_rey_to_release_lizzy_grant*
44. *https://www.rollingstone.com/music/music-news/lana-del-rey-to-re-release-first-album-236575/*
45. *https://www.mtv.com/news/2nps55/lana-del-rey-first-album-5-points-records-interview*
46. *https://www.rollingstone.com/music/music-news/18-things-you-learn-after-two-long-days-with-lana-del-rey-170579/*
47. *https://thequietus.com/articles/07106-lana-del-rey-interview*
48. GQ France according to *https://lanadelrey.fandom.com/wiki/Poolside_(film)*
49. *https://www.youtube.com/watch?v=zRAFNSgk1Ns*
50. *https://www.clashmusic.com/features/lana-del-rey-interview/*
51. *https://thequietus.com/articles/07106-lana-del-rey-interview*
52. *https://www.instagram.com/p/B3ffV0DnxQQ/*
53. *https://www.dazeddigital.com/music/article/33227/1/the-enduring-legacy-of-lana-del-rey-s-video-games*
54. *https://pitchfork.com/features/rising/8657-lana-del-rey/*
55. *https://www.gq-magazine.co.uk/article/woman-of-the-year-lana-del-rey*
56. *https://www.bbc.com/news/entertainment-arts-16729651*
57. *https://www.bbc.com/news/entertainment-arts-16729651*
58. *https://www.washingtonpost.com/graphics/2019/entertainment/lana-del-rey/*
59. *https://www.bbc.com/news/entertainment-arts-16729651*
60. *https://consequence.net/2011/10/quoteworthy-lana-del-rey-explains-name-change/*
61. *https://books.google.com.tw/books?id=RsAnJ7Zx_qgC&pg=RA2-PA8&lpg=RA2-PA8&d-q=%22And+if+I+gave+her+advice+on+dressing,+it+would+not+be+right.%22+la-na&source=bl&ots=_a1qcCp0Aa&sig=ACfU3U3Uv1A9GkUZvj228D9Y72qXjOPt-tw&hl=en&sa=X&ved=2ahUKEwiousel0LT9AhWjrlYBHVeNB2IQ6AF6BAgJEAM#v=o-nepage&q=%22And%20if%20I%20gave%20her%20advice%20on%20dressing%2C%20it%20would%20not%20be%20right.%22%20lana&f=false*
62. *https://www.mtv.com/news/2nps55/lana-del-rey-first-album-5-points-records-interview*
63. *https://www.smh.com.au/entertainment/music/lolita-in-the-hood-20140505-37r6n.html*
64. *https://i-d.vice.com/en/article/mbvjdp/the-greatest-lana-del-rey-songs-that-never-made-an-offi-cial-album*
65. *https://www.billboard.com/music/music-news/lana-del-rey-the-billboard-cover-story-512467/*

66. *https://www.youtube.com/watch?v=yb7VpH2QsxU*
67. *https://www.smh.com.au/entertainment/music/lolita-in-the-hood-20140505-37r6n.html*
68. *https://www.mtv.com/news/2nps55/lana-del-rey-first-album-5-points-records-interview*
69. *https://www.electronicbeats.net/lana-del-rey-interview/*
70. *https://www.complex.com/music/2011/12/lana-del-rey-the-hot-complex-gallery-interview*
71. *https://www.youtube.com/watch?v=tvVgzOwtTGY*
72. *https://www.smh.com.au/entertainment/music/lolita-in-the-hood-20140505-37r6n.html*
73. *https://www.digitalspy.com/music/a352467/lana-del-rey-people-didnt-take-me-seriously-with-a-high-voice/*
74. *https://twitter.com/elizadushku/status/158463989498654723?lang=en*
75. *https://www.hollywoodreporter.com/news/general-news/lana-del-rey-snl-juliette-lewis-slammed-twitter-281938/*
76. *https://www.yahoo.com/entertainment/lana-del-rey-recalls-her-133759407.html*
77. *https://www.cbsnews.com/news/daniel-radcliffe-defends-lana-del-reys-snl-performance/*
78. *https://www.dailymail.co.uk/tvshowbiz/article-7609661/Elton-John-discusses-Lana-Del-Rey-crucified-SNL-Rolling-Stone-magazine.html*
79. *https://popcrush.com/lana-del-rey-snl-performance-daniel-radcliffe-brian-williams/*
80. *https://www.hollywoodreporter.com/tv/tv-news/snl-kristen-wiigs-lana-del-rey-channing-tatum-287145/*
81. *https://www.gq-magazine.co.uk/article/woman-of-the-year-lana-del-rey*
82. *https://www.clashmusic.com/features/lana-del-rey-interview/*
83. *https://www.mtv.com/news/gcl0ps/actor-lana-del-rey-born-to-die-video*
84. *https://www.youtube.com/watch?v=zRAFNSgk1Ns*
85. *https://www.complex.com/music/lana-del-rey-interview-2017-cover-story*
86. *https://www.youtube.com/watch?v=XtNBRE9ffnE&t=2s*
87. *https://www.digitalspy.com/music/a404697/lana-del-rey-i-was-a-big-drinker-by-the-time-i-was-14/*
88. *https://www.youtube.com/watch?v=-7QwPDRP__o*
89. *https://www.huffpost.com/entry/interview-singersongwrite_b_159346*
90. *https://www.youtube.com/watch?v=zRAFNSgk1Ns*
91. *https://www.thenav.ca/2013/01/09/lana-del-ray/*
92. *https://web.archive.org/web/20131005012807/http://www.electronicbeats.net/en/features/interviews/lana-del-rey-interview/*
93. *https://www.youtube.com/watch?v=zRAFNSgk1Ns*
94. *https://www.youtube.com/watch?v=3DyLIqMCdj0*
95. *https://www.gq-magazine.co.uk/article/woman-of-the-year-lana-del-rey*
96. *https://www.bbc.com/news/entertainment-arts-16729651*
97. *https://www.bbc.com/news/entertainment-arts-16729651*
98. *https://www.youtube.com/watch?v=3DyLIqMCdj0*
99. *https://www.gq.com/story/lana-del-rey-interview-video-games*
100. *https://www.forbes.com/sites/hannahelliott/2012/08/22/jaguar-taps-lana-del-rey-for-f-type/?sh=1996622b5a34*
101. *https://media.jaguar.com/news/2013/02/lana-del-rey-releases-music-video-new-track-burning-desire*
102. *https://www.youtube.com/watch?v=e_X3fNFLYoE*
103. *https://news.yahoo.com/lana-del-rey-talks-idolizing-201449384.html*
104. *https://www.dazeddigital.com/music/article/14982/1/lana-del-rey-remixed-by-lindstrom*
105. *https://www.electronicbeats.net/lana-del-rey-interview/*
106. *https://www.interviewmagazine.com/music/lana-del-rey-and-billie-eilish-fall-in-love*
107. *https://www.nme.com/news/music/lana-del-rey-37-1207109*
108. *https://uk.style.yahoo.com/lana-del-rey-shading-her-120000103.html*
109. *https://www.bbc.com/news/entertainment-arts-16729651*
110. *https://www.teenvogue.com/story/lana-del-rey-trump*

111. https://www.nylon.com/entertainment/lana-del-rey-defends-her-music-against-abuse-glamori-zation-allegations
112. https://www.electronicbeats.net/lana-del-rey-interview/
113. https://www.electronicbeats.net/lana-del-rey-interview/
114. https://www.electronicbeats.net/lana-del-rey-interview/
115. https://www.nme.com/news/music/lana-del-rey-clarifies-trump-comments-taken-out-of-con-text-2854969
116. https://people.com/music/lana-del-rey-madness-trump-needed-happen-calls-capitol-riots-disas-sociated-rage/
117. https://sports.yahoo.com/lana-del-rey-doesn-t-182738675.html
118. https://www.insider.com/lana-del-rey-says-mask-had-plastic-underneath-2020-11
119. https://www.nme.com/news/music/you-need-an-intervention-lana-del-rey-hits-out-at-kanye-west-for-donald-trump-support-2385244
120. https://essentialsmagazine.com.au/people/sombre-lust-for-lana/
121. https://www.electronicbeats.net/lana-del-rey-interview/
122. https://www.electronicbeats.net/lana-del-rey-interview/
123. https://www.youtube.com/watch?v=e_X3fNFLYoE
124. https://www.independent.co.uk/arts-entertainment/music/features/lana-del-rey-independ-ence-day-blue-bannisters-b1876918.html
125. Del Rey talking to Alex Dyson of Breakfast with Tom and Alex.
126. https://lanadelrey.fandom.com/wiki/Young_and_Beautiful_(song)
127. https://www.hollywoodreporter.com/news/music-news/big-eyes-lana-del-rey-749904/
128. https://www.vogue.co.uk/article/lana-del-rey
129. https://www.dailymail.co.uk/tvshowbiz/article-2420993/Lana-Del-Rey-misses-mark-dated-double-denim-flashes-long-limbs-tiny-hot-pants.html
130. https://www.clashmusic.com/features/american-dreamer-lana-del-rey-interviewed
131. https://www.rollingstone.com/music/music-news/lana-del-reys-muse-is-very-fickle-74047/
132. http://underthegunreview.net/2013/08/16/lana-del-rey-claims-leaked-songs-are-due-to-a-hack-er/
133. https://www.datathistle.com/article/53977-lana-del-ray-feels-discouraged-since-song-leaks/amp/
134. https://www.culledculture.com/something-old-is-new-again-as-usual-lana-del-reys-elvis-and-the-king/
135. https://www.theguardian.com/music/2013/dec/05/lana-del-rey-new-album-title-ultraviolence
136. https://www.cbsnews.com/seattle/news/lana-del-rey-says-new-record-is-so-dark-its-almost-unlis-tenable/
137. https://essentialsmagazine.com.au/people/sombre-lust-for-lana/
138. https://essentialsmagazine.com.au/people/sombre-lust-for-lana/
139. https://www.idolator.com/7443878/lana-del-rey-new-album-spiritual-stripped-down-dark?chrome=1
140. https://www.gawker.com/lana-del-rey-thats-no-way-for-a-pop-star-to-behave-1592795627
141. https://soundcloud.com/lindzydelrey/lana-del-rey-interview-on-triple-j-radio-july-62014
142. https://www.youtube.com/watch?v=yb7VpH2QsxU
143. https://www.theguardian.com/music/2020/may/21/lana-del-rey-hits-back-at-critics-who-say-she-glamorises-abuse
144. https://faroutmagazine.co.uk/lana-del-rey-lyric-regret/
145. https://pitchfork.com/news/55558-lana-del-rey-says-lou-reed-died-the-day-they-were-supposed-to-record-brooklyn-baby-together/
146. https://soundcloud.com/ldrfancom/ultraviolence-ldr-commentary
147. https://www.npr.org/2014/06/21/323209791/lana-del-rey-i-dont-have-other-people-in-mind
148. https://rockcelebrities.net/the-truth-about-axl-rose-and-lana-del-rey-relationship/
149. https://pitchfork.com/features/rising/8657-lana-del-rey/
150. https://outofshell.tistory.com/m/625
151. https://www.smh.com.au/entertainment/music/lolita-in-the-hood-20140505-37r6n.html

152. https://www.billboard.com/music/music-news/marilyn-manson-eli-roth-lana-del-rey-video-explanation-6405571/
153. https://www.gawker.com/marilyn-manson-explains-the-infamous-leaked-lana-del-re-1669910813
154. https://completemusicupdate.com/article/marilyn-manson-speaks-on-lana-del-rey-rape-video/
155. https://faroutmagazine.co.uk/courtney-love-favourite-lana-del-rey-song/
156. https://www.dazeddigital.com/music/article/35578/1/lana-del-rey-courtney-love-lust-for-life
157. https://www.theguardian.com/music/2014/jun/12/lana-del-rey-ultraviolence-album
158. https://pitchfork.com/news/55670-frances-bean-cobain-to-lana-del-rey-the-death-of-young-musicians-isnt-something-to-romanticize/
159. https://www.rollingstone.com/music/music-news/frances-bean-cobain-to-lana-del-rey-early-death-isnt-cool-84819/
160. https://www.complex.com/music/2012/01/lana-del-rey-2012-cover-story
161. Del Rey talking to Triple J of ABC News Australia
162. https://www.youtube.com/watch?v=rmWeiOfhdRg
163. https://www.digitalspy.com/music/v-festival/a665218/mark-ronson-wont-be-on-lana-del-reys-album-i-hate-to-crap-all-over-your-excitement/
164. https://www.youtube.com/watch?v=XtNBRE9ffnE&t
165. https://www.youtube.com/watch?v=XtNBRE9ffnE&t=2s
166. https://www.huffpost.com/entry/lana-del-rey-honeymoon_n_55a557aae4b0ecec71bd3714
167. https://www.thecurrent.org/feature/2015/11/10/lana-del-rey-on-paranoia-father-john-misty-nina-simone-and-honeymoon
168. https://soundcloud.com/lananow/music-to-watch-boys-to
169. https://www.digitalspy.com/music/a619243/lana-del-rey-reveals-title-of-new-track-talks-big-eyes-inspiration/
170. https://www.nme.com/features/a-letter-from-lana-del-rey-the-full-nme-cover-interview-757009
171. https://www.youtube.com/watch?v=XtNBRE9ffnE&t=2s
172. https://pitchfork.com/news/61207-lana-del-rey-shares-salvatore/
173. https://www.wmagazine.com/life/lana-del-rey-new-album-music-interview-2022
174. https://faroutmagazine.co.uk/lana-del-reys-cover-of-daniel-johnston/
175. https://www.billboard.com/music/music-news/lana-del-rey-daniel-johnston-hi-how-are-you-daniel-johnston-short-film-premiere-6754166/
176. https://www.billboard.com/music/music-news/lana-del-rey-daniel-johnston-hi-how-are-you-daniel-johnston-short-film-premiere-6754166/
177. https://www.youtube.com/watch?v=mnU01_rw_AY
178. https://pitchfork.com/features/interview/9711-the-dark-knight-returns-a-conversation-with-the-weeknd/?page=1
179. https://www.her.ie/celeb/james-franco-has-opened-up-about-his-relationship-with-lana-del-rey-208808
180. https://www.nme.com/news/music/lana-del-rey-42-1224037
181. https://www.youtube.com/watch?v=iIY1hDWz_-c
182. https://www.vulture.com/2017/02/watch-lana-del-reys-new-music-video-for-love.html
183. https://www.nme.com/news/music/lana-del-rey-sean-ono-lennon-collaboration-2054352#SyIZEWsUvGK76Bd9.99
184. https://www.dazeddigital.com/music/article/35578/1/lana-del-rey-courtney-love-lust-for-life
185. https://www.vulture.com/2017/04/lana-del-rey-wrote-a-song-on-the-way-home-from-coachella.html
186. https://www.complex.com/music/2017/05/lana-del-rey-coachella-woodstock-in-my-mind
187. https://genius.com/a/songwriter-producer-rick-nowels-explains-how-lana-del-rey-s-lust-for-life-came-together
188. https://www.standard.co.uk/showbiz/celebrity-news/lana-del-rey-warns-to-steer-clear-of-selfish-singers-and-date-a-bassist-a3536126.html

189. *https://www.flaunt.com/content/people/lana-del-rey*
190. *https://archive.flaunt.com/content/people/lana-del-rey*
191. *https://www.youtube.com/watch?v=9glg0Tx4trA*
192. *https://www.nme.com/news/music/lana-del-rey-sean-ono-lennon-collaboration-2054352*
193. *https://www.flaunt.com/content/people/lana-del-rey*
194. *https://www.lanadelreyfan.com/lana-del-rey-talks-to-swedish-magazine-bon-i-love-my-work-and-what-i-do/*
195. *https://www.youtube.com/watch?v=SQgYaSGlQjM*
196. *https://www.npr.org/sections/world-cafe/2018/02/16/586059115/lana-del-rey-on-world-cafe*
197. *https://www.stereogum.com/1944688/watch-lana-del-rey-tease-new-song-with-aap-rocky-and-playboi-carti/news/*
198. *https://www.rollingstone.com/music/music-news/watch-lana-del-rey-talk-potential-radiohead-lawsuit-at-denver-concert-124011/*
199. *https://www.billboard.com/music/rock/radiohead-publisher-lana-del-rey-creep-negotiations-8093395/*
200. *https://www.youtube.com/watch?v=Fi66v0Nqo34*
201. *https://www.nme.com/big-reads/lana-del-rey-interview-normal-rockwell-big-read-2544895*
202. *https://www.thefader.com/2018/03/05/lana-del-rey-you-must-love-me-cover*
203. *https://gagadaily.com/forums/topic/286856-lana-del-r-for-i-d-magazine-gucci/*
204. *https://www.vanityfair.com/style/2019/08/lana-del-rey-new-album-2020*
205. *https://faroutmagazine.co.uk/hear-lana-del-reys-isolated-vocals-for-mariners-apartment-complex/*
206. *https://www.nme.com/news/music/lana-del-rey-album-venice-bitch-video-2380471*
207. *https://i-d.vice.com/en/article/mbzg48/lana-del-rey-interview-gucci-guilty-album-norman-rockwell*
208. *https://www.billboard.com/music/pop/lana-del-rey-billboard-cover-story-2019-8527901/*
209. *https://www.youtube.com/watch?v=lvRgB4lNoCg*
210. *https://www.washingtonpost.com/graphics/2019/entertainment/lana-del-rey/*
211. *https://pitchfork.com/news/lana-del-rey-teases-new-song-venice-bitch-listen/*
212. *Instagram livestream on September 4, 2019 according to https://lanadelrey.fandom.com/wiki/Love_Song_(song)*
213. *https://www.npr.org/2019/09/04/757545360/lana-del-rey-lives-in-americas-messy-subconscious*
214. *https://www.latimes.com/entertainment-arts/story/2019-09-05/lana-del-rey-norman-rockwell-npr*
215. *https://www.youtube.com/watch?v=mF-83JPKX60*
216. *https://www.complex.com/music/2019/08/lana-del-rey-wasnt-sold-working-with-jack-antonoff-new-album*
217. *https://abbeyroadinstitute.nl/blog/jack-antonoff-brutal-honesty/*
218. *https://i-d.vice.com/en/article/mbzg48/lana-del-rey-interview-gucci-guilty-album-norman-rockwell*
219. *https://www.youtube.com/watch?v=iIY1hDWz_-c&t=1s*
220. *https://www.stereogum.com/2056648/lana-del-rey-says-shes-working-on-another-new-album-called-white-hot-forever/news/*
221. *https://www.youtube.com/shorts/tbcigzr-3cs*
222. *https://www.complex.com/music/2020/11/lana-del-rey-responds-mesh-mask-controversy*
223. *https://www.liverpoolfc.com/news/first-team/130816-photos-lana-del-rey-at-anfield*
224. *https://www.rollingstone.com/music/music-news/lana-del-rey-joni-mitchell-for-free-894246/*
225. *https://www.nme.com/news/music/lana-del-rey-teases-music-video-norman-fucking-rockwell-2544046*
226. *https://www.pmstudio.com/music/music.html?page=20210112-12903*
227. *https://www.interviewmagazine.com/music/who-is-lana-del-rey-jack-antonoff-september-poetry-cover*

228. https://www.youtube.com/watch?v=1Qw0Mll7tjo
229. https://www.vulture.com/2021/01/lana-del-rey-reveals-chemtrails-over-the-country-club-cover.html
230. https://www.stereogum.com/2112570/lana-del-rey-chemtrails-country-club-artwork-tracklist/news/
231. https://ew.com/music/lana-del-rey-clarifies-trump-capitol-riots/
232. https://www.interviewmagazine.com/music/who-is-lana-del-rey-jack-antonoff-september-poetry-cover
233. https://www.billboard.com/music/pop/lana-del-rey-sling-ice-skating-accident-9504851/
234. https://faroutmagazine.co.uk/lana-del-rey-song-inspired-madonna-party/
235. https://faroutmagazine.co.uk/nightmare-encounter-with-hero-inspired-lana-del-rey/
236. BBC Radio 1 on April 19, 2017 according to https://lanadelrey.fandom.com/wiki/Yosemite_(song)
237. https://www.yahoo.com/entertainment/nikki-lane-working-lana-del-133534272.html
238. https://www.dazeddigital.com/music/article/54099/1/lana-del-rey-explains-why-shes-quitting-deactivating-social-media-blue-banisters
239. https://www.nme.com/news/music/lana-del-rey-announces-new-album-rock-candy-sweet-2904630
240. https://www.rollingstone.co.uk/music/features/lana-del-rey-she-does-it-for-the-girls-album-27426
241. https://faroutmagazine.co.uk/lana-del-rey-artist-changed-contemporary-music/
242. https://www.youtube.com/watch?v=4alfkfM_Hdc
243. https://patriotla.iheart.com/alternate/amp/2022-10-19-lana-del-rey-says-laptop-containing-new-music-book-was-stolen/
244. https://hypebae.com/2022/10/lana-del-rey-unreleased-music-album-book-poetry-stolen
245. https://www.nme.com/news/music/lana-del-rey-wishes-she-had-sung-the-entire-second-verse-on-taylor-swifts-snow-on-the-beach-3404998
246. https://www.interviewmagazine.com/music/lana-del-rey-and-billie-eilish-fall-in-love
247. https://www.billboard.com/music/music-news/lana-del-rey-family-tunnel-under-ocean-blvd-album-1235258689/
248. https://www.iheart.com/content/2022-12-02-lana-del-rey-just-teased-a-massive-announcement/
249. https://www.billboard.com/music/music-news/lana-del-rey-aw-new-song-1235253800/
250. https://www.rollingstone.com/music/music-news/lana-del-rey-dad-rob-grant-announces-album-lost-at-sea-1234685722/
251. https://www.rollingstone.co.uk/music/features/lana-del-rey-she-does-it-for-the-girls-album-27426/
252. https://www.billboard.com/music/awards/lana-del-rey-billboard-women-in-music-speech-full-1235278112/
253. https://www.youtube.com/shorts/jeNjlB8IflU
254. https://www.nme.com/en_asia/news/music/bruce-springsteen-lana-del-rey-simply-best-songwriters-us-2729066
255. https://www.nme.com/news/music/courtney-love-says-kurt-cobain-and-lana-del-ray-are-the-only-true-musical-geniuses-shes-ever-known-3372057
256. https://hypebae.com/2023/2/lana-del-rey-taylor-swift-collab-snow-on-the-beach-explanation
257. https://www.rollingstone.com/music/music-features/elton-john-lana-del-rey-musicians-on-musicians-cover-902354/
258. https://www.rollingstone.com/music/music-features/adele-inside-her-private-life-and-triumphant-return-37131/
259. https://www.billboard.com/music/pop/father-john-misty-covers-lana-del-rey-ride-video-8379660/
260. https://www.youtube.com/watch?v=-7QwPDRP__o

*F\*\*ked My Way Up to the Top: The Complete Biography of Lana Del Rey Using Her Own Words*
by Jared Woods
co-editing by Milz Dechnik
Published by The Goat's Nest Publishing
ISBN 9798386871697
**JaredWoodsSavedMyLife.com**